A WOMAN'S PRIMER

First published 2014 by Shadow Teams.

Powered by

SHADOW
TEAMS

RUTH SIDRANSKY

An Invitation to Life, Love & Work

A WOMAN'S PRIMER

To Gina & Freddie —
With love always —
Your sister

Ruth Sidransky

10/25/2015

For Sarah, Rachel and Carrie

Acknowledgments:

There are many to thank, but above all my son Mark who began this publication process by sending off this manuscript, initially, without my permission, as it was meant for family and friends only. He persuaded me, convincing me by the words, "Others have gone through this, others are going through this, and will find comfort knowing they are not alone."

And then there is Beth Wareham, editor and publisher who guided me through the maze of twenty-first century publishing both on the Internet and in print, taking me farther and farther afield into technocracy. I owe her an enormous debt.

Contents

Women are amazing.

Thus begins the entry for the letter "A" in Ruth Sidransky's glorious <u>Primer</u>, a journey through fragments of a long life that examines the unique strength of women through every part of the passage, ordinary days and extraordinary ones, difficulties and joy, sorrow and triumphs.

Like the powerfully observed worlds of Annie Dillard and fearless inquiry of Joan Didion, Sidranksy looks into the beauty of the world as well as its dangers. Her language is as sharp as saw grass, her observations surprising and always profound. And when the grass leaves marks, Sidransky helps the wounded march through it and on, healing as they go.

What of Sidransky's choices for the letters of <u>A Woman's Primer</u>? What words do young women need to keep close their chests as the run through the field of the living, hearts open and filled with awe?

All women must be brave. The world will throw powerful events toward each woman that she must address and overcome. She will meet love and learn to listen to its languages and meaning, learn to trust herself and her instincts. Kindness, safety, a sense of purpose and the comfort of family are also monumental in the lives of women.

Sidransky, now 85, reaches into her life's long arc and finds modern pragmatism: Women need financial independence, meaningful work, jobs, respect, careers, healthcare, childcare, freedom of body and freedom of thought. In her 90th decade, <u>A Woman's Primer</u> is one of three books she will publish this year.

Part memoir, part philosophical inquiry into the soul of women, Sidransky affirms the journey through it all, finally accepting that life exists for life itself, for the daffodil that comes up yellow every spring.

Here is **A Woman's Primer**, the ABC's of a life, of a woman beginning again and again.

Introduction

Women are amazing.

Our lives intersect throughout every phase of time's passage: birth to death, and all the living in between, our first day at school, best friends in adolescence, the first kiss, the thrill of falling in love, marriage, children, careers, divorce, illness, and the final end game when we might wonder if we did justice to the life granted us.

Life lived is lived in women's wisdom, in women's talk, in women's sharing. We do better with one another, have difficulty without each other. Often we share intimacies of life with a trusted friend. Sometimes a passing stranger will offer lifelong advice; sometimes a close friend will proffer a hand without being asked, and sometimes it's just about giggles, the sheer pleasure of each other's company.

So without a prior plan this book evolved, fell out of my hands, a primer for women, an ABC of women's attributes, power, feelings, emotions and thoughts. There is much to write, and I offer stories, fragments of my life as a measure of the way in which l lived, sometimes with careful planning and some-times wherever the wind and rain, sun and warmth invited me, wherever random chance found me. I lived at times with daring and always with amazing discovery for the small and the large, for the seemingly unimportant and the important markers of life from birth to death.

So it is with women, most women. We begin to fathom love's importance with the touch of our mother's hands from babyhood on. I had 'touch' much longer than most. I had my mother's touch well into my adulthood. I had it even in the days when she was hobbled by a stroke and confined to a nursing home bed. I'd pick up her hand and stroke my face with it and she'd smile a crooked smile. And when she lay dead, I lifted her hand to my face, once more, to feel her. She was my mother and I am mother to my children, and grandmother to my grandchildren. The root source of my life as a woman was my mother. She was and continues to be the source of daily renewal.

My mother Mary was different than most, her language was different. She was born deaf and Signed, spoke and wrote fractured English. When things were difficult, when my daughter was diagnosed with second stage lymphoma, when her husband walked out on her care, I left my home, my husband and my widowed mother who lived alone, flew to Los Angeles, California to care for my adult daughter. My mother typed in bright green capital letters on her TTY (telephone typewriter) words that flashed before me, four words that read "*TAKE EASY TAKE BRAVE*".

So simple. Her English had her own syntax, her meaning absolutely clear. We do not speak of bravery today, but it does take bravery to deal with life crises. And with it comes the ability to take it easy, to relax. It is a matter of self-preservation.

Yet, my mother had that twinkle, that grin, that smile that said, "Here I am, happy." Not always, certainly. But the new day was welcomed, and we as children, my younger brother and I, were told to look out the window at the wonder of the new dawning day. She was functionally illiterate, yet wise about celebrating the ordinariness of each day.

"To celebrate" is the infinitive of the verb. It is a verb that we ordinarily use in conjunction with a holiday, with days especially marked on the calendar. Each day is a wonder, a cause for celebration.

My mother, locked in silence, was acutely aware of the world around her, of the streets where she lived, of the stores in which she shopped, of the people who passed her by without so much of a thought of her beauty. She had sharp eyes; she was witness to the life milling about in her daily orbit. One might say the circumference of her days was a small one, a narrow one. But then, don't we all choose a daily path and trod it without conscious effort, without continual decision making as to our steps to this place and that place?

She was one of a small group of people gifted with acute awareness, gathering impressions to take home, to tell her family of the richness of her day. She shared the humor or sadness of her moments outside the confines of our small Bronx, New York apartment with great pleasure and then enjoined us to 'eat something' to stave off our childhood hunger. Her face lit up, her smile crinkled around her mouth, her eyes shone and her hands Signed, "See, now we have a party!"

Perhaps she never knew the exact linguistic nuance of the verb 'to celebrate', but she knew *how* to celebrate. She was a woman blessed with innate joy. Yet, like all women, like all people, of all languages, or all religions, she had her life's difficulties and tragedies. I've seen her weep and I've seen her smile. And I know that she, as a woman, had the capacity to shake off the 'hardness' of her life and continue for the sake of her own life and the lives of her family.

Because she was deaf, because language and all it imparts was in her hands, she quite naturally used her hands in space to communicate a thought, a wish. She touched me. Her hand on my shoulder, on my back, on the top of my head, on my cheek, on my face…all of it touched me, separated me from the essential scourge of the human being, separated me from loneliness, from aloneness.

My mother touched me; my mother loved me.

When my father died my mother was at my side. I had to tell her that her Benny was gone. Her first words were, "Who will make me laugh?" The two of them, my wonderful parents had a secret. A simple secret. Laughter and humor were gifts they shared to take the sting out of life's silences. They gifted that charming wisdom to me. They taught me to receive humor with delight.

They cautioned me against taking the aging process too seriously. I have asked myself, as many must do, how did I reach this age without recognition that it would come, that I would see the flaking of my skin, or the wrinkles that appear without warning on my once smooth face, that I would look in the mirror and see my aging mother? Me?

The doorbell rings. The deliveryman interrupts my concern over time's passage. He ignores my obvious annoyance and loads a large package into my arms. I say, "I'm an old lady. I don't know if I can carry this."

He grins a wide smile and says, "The older the moon, the brighter it shines."

"Who told you that?"

"My Jamaican grandfather."

He turns away and walks to his small yellow van and winks at me. "You ain't no old lady. You're a grand woman."

He tickles my soul.

Woman, indeed!

A moment of levity. A break in the day. And they do come, sometimes often, sometimes a dry spell. Humor promised is a life gain. At last a man that knows a woman.

Women are crucial for the continuation of life, for offering their secrets to their young, for nurturing the young to adolescence and finally to adulthood. It is so in every culture: Western, Oriental, Latin, tribal. Producing babies is beyond the menopausal woman, but imparting wisdom gleaned from life is not beyond her capacity. Not beyond a grandmother's teachings.

I do believe the place to begin is in a woman's body. We must, as women, take care of ourselves first, and then care for the others in our lives. Bodies have a life of their own. We disregard our bodies at our peril. Nourish that body, some would say, that God-given body. Whatever the genesis, it is my body, your body, to care for. Treat it lovingly, for 'it' is more than an 'it'. It houses the sum of you, of me. Tend it wisely; give it a long and healthy life. It is the pathway to your soul, to your very heartbeat. It is your body that begins your day, your arms and legs as they stretch out of bed, and as you move about on your ordinary/extraordinary life. One day all the care, all the activity of life stops. You and your body are gone from gracing the earth with your footsteps. Your plans, your dreams and desires are done. And I remember John Donne's words:

> Death be not proud, though some shall call thee
> Mighty and dreadful, for thou art not so

Live life each day. Be glad. Be sad if you must. Death is that unknown quantity, that unknown place, without clear definition. So live! Treat yourself with humor and delight, be serious, be generous, love your children, your partner, your family, love yourself, for you above all need care. Smile, laugh, giggle and say "No!' to all the naysayers who would thwart your dreams. Walk with your head high! And if you can no longer walk, ride high.

Our bodies, particularly when we are in good health, house our minds to the optimum: our thoughts, our feelings and often our sadly maligned emotions. Women are not merely a conglomerate of reproductive organs designed to keep the human species from extinction. We have enormous value beyond the baby bearing years. I look to the grandmothers across cultures who take care of the young, who hand down the lore of their ancestors, who teach the young mothers and their young children, each in their own way the continuity and joy of life. Yes, there is sorrow and tragedy and blank days and boredom for some, but it is all life. Today, there are single women, women without children, and they too have, even as they age, a significant role in society.

More and more is expected of women. In some families, we are the breadwinners in whatever sphere our working lives take us. Without question, we still are expected to give birth and rear a family with or without outside help.

I say, 'Help!'

Decade by decade, the life span of women increases. Women must lead in finding ways to use the added years given to them. If I continue the ceaseless striving to find meaning I will find, at least for me, a dead end. I can only know what each day brings and find cause to celebrate the day: a stroll down the street, a nod to a neighbor, the nuzzle of big blonde Labrador retriever, a telephone call from a friend, from one of my adult children and a myriad of small and large events of the day. It is the *ordinary* from which I take comfort.

After all the searching, all the planning, it becomes that simple. As I walked this morning past an outdoor café, there was a beautiful female bull mastiff with floppy ears seated upright next to her master scanning the passersby. I stopped and offered

my hand under her wet black nose. She sniffed: this big creature. Suddenly, without a signal from me she offered me one
paw and then the other. I smiled. It's the ordinary that becomes
extraordinary. It is the small gesture that becomes large; it is a
pure moment of happiness. I shall remember this huge tame
tawny animal for days and weeks to come and remember the
moment of unexpected pleasure.

One might scoff at this particular pleasure as a bit of fluff. It
is not. It is part of the makeup of one's day, of one's life. Mine.

It was akin to my children's laughter when they were small.
To hear a nine-month old baby deliver a rolling belly laugh at
some silly paternal antic set the day's pattern for me. I am sure
I am not alone in the delight of life's apparent small gifts. They
do constitute life's meaning in unknown ways: in our emotional
well-being, in our own smiles, in the way we construct our
everyday experiences.

They offer moments of awe, if we but notice.

Small pleasures, small gifts do add up to life's joy.

I do not deny the tragedies that can and do befall us. They
are there. They are strong. They are counteracted with the small
smile, with the gesture of one human being to another, with
human touch. Life is a medley of events that season us as people. People to people, parent to child, child to parent, it is all
part of the weaving, part of the memory that create us. It is
human history or *her*story.

I am a writer. I love writing. I find pleasure in the process. At
times it frustrates me, but most often the flow is unstoppable.

I cannot write without imagination, without inspiration and above all without memory, whether it is my own memory, or the memory found in the pages of a book, or the oral memory of others.

Louis Buñuel, the filmmaker, wrote in <u>My Last Sight</u>, "One has to begin to lose memory, even small fragments of it, to realize that memory is what our entire life is made of. A life without memory wouldn't be life, as an intelligence without means of expression wouldn't be intelligence. Our memory is our coherence, our reason, our action, our feeling. Without it we aren't anything."

We must remember to search out a life of our own, to create our own memories, each of us in our own way. Memory is fragmented. Our lives are fragmented. Particularly for women, for those with families and those without.

I spend my summers in Western Massachusetts and the last days of summer have arrived. I watch the tips of the northern trees turn into shades of gold. Not yet, not yet, I murmur softly. How did the summer dissolve into September? The sun has risen, the air is cool; the land shines with early morning dew, each blade of grass defined in the bright light of morning. The house is still. And I await the unfolding day in awe. A new season is upon the land. An ordinary day. So we begin. Life.

Yet as the year ages, we humans age. I age. We must confront death. I am deeply connected to my mother.

What of women who face their wrinkled necks? What of the aging process?

I was connected to her aging process and my own. My mother claimed her birthday was March 6, 1908, but when she and my father inquired by writing notes, (English Sign Language and American Sign Language are not compatible), at the Hall of Public Records in White Chapel, London, England, in the summer of 1959, she was told that she was born on April 10,1908. I shall never know the exact date of her arrival on Earth. She died on November 1,1989 and with her went the untold stories of her life.

It is not aging I fear; it is death, that unknown void. When I sleep I dream. The brain functions. There is pleasure in sleep: the bedtime ritual, the ablutions before sliding under the clean sheets, the blanket, the pulling up of the comforter on a cold winter's evening, the punching down of the pillow, the exact spot on which I lay my head, the turning over onto my right side, curled almost fetal, closing my eyes, and slipping away to deep rest (away with the fairies), knowing I will awaken in the morning to a blue sky stained with a pale moon remnant, the stretching before arising; these are but a few of the pleasures of sleep.

There is no rising from death; there is no morning bird song, no hum of the tea-kettle, no preparation for the day to come—no daily ritual. It is done. Life is done. There is nothing. A tombstone perhaps. Memory of those who lived, memory granted to those who live on, only memory. And then is it truly ended?

I have no answers. Shall I ask God? Hello God, what is the

measure of a man's life, of a woman's life? How shall you, the reader, determine that measure, that quality?

What of the years before the end? What preparation then? 'The quality of life', that phrase bandied about, written about, mouthed so often seems to be without substance. Who decides what that quality is? Is not one birdsong a day enough, a call to live, to be lived, or remembered?

I go to the synagogue nearest my home on occasional Saturday mornings. So many are old, in varying stages of decrepitude. For the first moments it is disconcerting to see them gripped in age, but I quickly understand they are living life as they are *able* to live it. They come to worship in community; they come to live. Hoorah!

I do not know how to be old. I am both young and old. I have the passion of the young, the driving intensity that held me in thrall all my life. That intensity never lets go of my soul. I have the resignation and fatigue of the old, at times the acceptance.

I had a violent dream, an arched black cat—not kitten, not yet adult, standing on a glacial blue ice sheet against the backdrop of the black night, an image, nothing more, but frightening enough to startle me awake. Does that dream belong on this page? Somehow, yes!

I am compelled by my spirit, my duende, my daimon, to write, to put pen to paper to tell stories mine, perhaps yours.

I am young.

I do not know how to be old.

Will I sleep one day and not awaken? When will my life end? Incomplete? Is life ever complete? I do not know.

In between life and death there is life, life, glorious life for all of us. And stories to be told.

I am in awe.

The Letter "A"

AWE

I begin with the letter **A.**

I am in awe of beginnings. I reach for beginnings. I am in awe of daybreak, in awe of the Eastern rising sun streaming light onto my desk. I am in awe of birth, the birth of life, of the story of Genesis, which speaks to beginnings. I am in awe of death, co-mingled with a touch of fear of the unknown.

Yes, I am in awe. The awe of life itself. We are given the words "fear God" in prayer, but I prefer the word 'awe'. I am in awe of the mystery of life. Perhaps there is no mystery, only life: gorgeous, crazy, frightening, fragmented wonderful life.

My mother, Mary and my father, Benny must have felt the promise when I was born. A hearing child, with all the wonder of sound, the wonder of a world they never knew or could ever know, the wonder of the sound of the human voice, the wonder of music, the wonder of eggs crackling in a frying pan and on and on. I was both their promise for entry into the hearing world, and I was the mystery they never quite fathomed.

I am in awe of how they managed, especially in the first days of my life, the first days at home, to raise me, not able to hear either a whimper or a prolonged cry. I am in awe of the human spirit that dares to bring life, missing a critical sense, particularly in the year that I was born, in the years of my childhood.

They did the ordinary. They fed me, they clothed me, they bathed me. My mother was 21 when I was born, my father 26, both devoid of fluent oral language. Yet, with trial and error they persevered. There are stories of my father scrubbing my eight-month-old back in the kitchen sink, oblivious to my cries until my paternal grandmother, who lived downstairs in her own apartment, came to rescue me from my screeching. There are stories of my mother staying awake in the early days of my infancy, watching me as I slept, lest she miss my cry for hunger. The stories abound, but they were all laced with care and love. Clearly, the saving grace of my childhood. They were in awe of me, their magical child, and I of them, who managed the ordinary with paucity of language.

My first language was Sign. I learned the homemade signs of my parent's day-to-day conversation. I learned the signs they taught to one another growing up in their respective schools. I learned new signs as they learned them from their more educated friends. I learned new signs as I watch the Deaf in our neighborhood gather on Bronx street corners on warm summer evenings. I learned new signs from other Deaf as they collected on the beaches of Coney Island and formed a circle of ten, twenty, often as many as thirty people, all signing in plain view of the others. I had never seen these Signs but inferred their meaning from the rest of the rapid sentences signed into space for everyone to see. They had no need of a microphone to be heard. They had their eyes and their uncanny sensibility to garner meaning, one from the other. Their humor was encased in body language, all the more amusing and so they laughed. Me too.

Standing alone among the Deaf, when I was in my early teens, I understood the connection of thousands of Deaf who lived before me, before my parents who made small and then large strides to create a common language. It was not until almost the end of the twentieth century that American Sign Language was recognized by the public at large, by a law enacted by Congress, that I now see interpreters signing the oral words of another in a small circle on the television screen. To cite a common cliché: wonder of wonders.

Sign language was forbidden to my mother and to my father in the public schools they attended. My mother, as did her deaf sister and brother, boarded at the Lexington School for the Deaf, and my father was a day student at P.S. 23, for 'hard of hearing' boys and girls. The terminology today is different. Sign is now, strange as it seems to write, a *legal* language, so declared by the American Disabilities Act of 1990. Today, Sign language is a credited course in many high schools and universities. Pediatricians advise young hearing mothers to Sign to their babies, citing the babies capacity to understand sign and sign themselves before their vocal chords are fully developed for speech. It is fun for me to sign to a hearing baby and watch the response. It is delightful to watch tiny fingers attempt intelligible sign. I do understand the baby as my mother understood me, signing as early as eleven months. So she said.

Then, in the first decade of the twentieth century, my parents and their classmates were punished for signing words created by past students or words they made up themselves. In both schools, teachers rapped the children's hands with a three-foot wooden ruler, sometimes until they were red. My mother was often afraid to sign.

So the young people would sign under school stairwells, or on street corners well away from the school buildings. It is hard to imagine language forbidden to a young child who could not grasp words on talking lips. I have tried. It is difficult, at times, impossible to understand, particularly if the speaker turns his head, or mumbles, or speaks with pursed lips.

To this day, there is still a contingent of educators who insist on teaching oral language exclusively to profoundly deaf children, and so these young people belong to neither world, neither to the deaf nor the hearing world, where they can be completely at ease and fluent in communicating with another person. I have often countered their unbending stand to create normalcy with the words to these well-intentioned educators: "Would you deny a blind child Braille?"

Language is, for me, man's greatest gift. Before the temple of language, I am awestruck.

My fingers fly on the computer, kinetic memory allows my thoughts to percolate down to the keyboard and write these words for another, for you, to read. Without language there is no complex thought. I did ask my father, who was keenly interested in the meaning of words, how he thought before he had no words to use as thinking tools. His answer was direct. "I thought in pictures," his hands flashed. Words were put into his toolbox for human contact, much as his toolbox of hammers, needles, thread and tacks served him as an upholsterer.

Language is the connecting link from one to another. It is language that teaches, that preaches, that sings, that develops science, that allows man and woman, child and adolescent to communicate thoughts of love, of worry, of anger, of war, of politics, of literature, of the field of psychology, of 'talk-ther-apy', of all scientific progress, of medicine, of technical data that advances day by day, of all new creations, and the list goes on and on. It matters not the language, be it Chinese, Spanish, French, German, English or some obscure dialect. Words form sentences, sentences form paragraphs of thought, and so we humans connect, from the cooing and sometimes seemingly silly sounds we make to our babies, to love making and to the technical thoughts in scientific laboratories and all the thoughts that we are heir to. The possibilities of language are endless. Therein lies yet another mystery: the power of the human mind to advance the limits of life as we know it today.

Language is tangible for the blind deaf. They touch for lan-guage, feeling the signs of another, their understanding com-pletely tactile, fingertip knowing. I have communicated fully with a blind deaf friend and seen comprehension, a moment of pleasure, a nodding of her head, and still wonder at the capacity of the human soul to connect with another. And Helen, that is her name, waits for my response to her words drawn into her palm so that she can know what I have to say. That is a mystery that I have never fathomed.

Language helps us heal, helps us to understand how to live. Language offers comfort in times of sorrow; language offers jubilation in times of great happiness.

Some live well, some do not. And somehow, language and the thought it engenders enters into the equation of life patterns. *I can't do* becomes *I can do*. I am in awe of blind hearing children who *do*, blind children who use listening to language to their advantage, leaving darkness behind them. Although it seems strange to put on the page, oral language permits the blind to see as only they can see, as only they can conjure physicality.

I had arranged for blind children to learn how to ride a horse. Impossible. Not at all. My Canadian husband and I lived in Toronto for many years. He and his partners owned a ranch outside the town of Orangeville, about an hour's drive from the city. There were 50 horses. One of the partners ran the ranch as a summer riding camp for children. And I, a trained teacher and administrator planned for the usage of the property year round, particularly for city children who had never left the confines of the concrete streets, who had never seen a cow or a rabbit run free across a meadow. We would teach children to ride a horse, to feel the warm flesh of a living animal beneath their bodies.

Of all the children we taught to ride, to feel a 1500 pound

animal in their control, none was more wondrous than teaching blind children to ride, to see them mount, to see their trepidation, to know their courage and then to see a smile across a young blind face as the horse moved forward, guided by a ranch hand, to see their small hands grip the worn leather reins, to smile to myself and say inwardly, "Good! They made it!" as they, a group of 6 blind children, and their horses walked down the pebbled path. There was pure glee on each face. And then, after the long ride, when they were allowed to ride without a guiding hand, the moment of disappointment arrived when, at last, they were helped to dismount. To reach out to these children, to give them the gift of control was reward enough for one outing. The buzz of excitement as these ten and twelve year olds dismounted was thrilling. They were aglow with success. They had conquered the language of touch; they had a life changing experience, a memory to hold. They were in awe of their own power.

They were their own blessing, and they blessed me in turn with their stalwart bravery. Not one blind child asked to be excused. Each child stood before his or her horse and with their small hands delivered a whole apple to each 1500-pound animal. For me, it was reward enough to see their ecstatic faces in the face of the enormous feat they each accomplished.

The Letter "B"

BRAVERY

May God bless you and guard you.
May God show you favor and be gracious to you.
May God show you kindness and grant you peace.

My mother never heard a Hebrew word, never understood the prayers in the synagogue. Yet she blessed me as a priest would. She raised her hand for the word God, and then with arms raised, all her fingers pinched together, she opened them softly and orally said the words, "Bless you", showering her mother's blessing over my head.

When my adult daughter lay half asleep in the Cancer Center at Cedars Sinai Hospital in Los Angeles receiving the poisonous, life saving drugs into her body I, too, would quietly bless her in Sign language, remembering my mother's blessing for me. The ritual of benediction was soothing; it was private and it was prayer. Each patient had a separate cubicle in the chemotherapy treatment center. Was my daughter conscious of my blessing? I believe so, but I cannot say with certainty. The bravery was hers; I offered the blessing, for her, for me.

At times I would sit silently beside other parents, other family members, and murmur some of the words of Psalm 91 to quiet my anxiety, my fear for her life force. *He will cover you with his pinions, and under his wings will you find refuge. His truth will be your shield and buckler. You will not be afraid of the terror by night; nor of the arrow that flies by day; nor of the pestilence that walks in darkness; nor of the destruction that wastes at noonday.*

I would know not only the strength of love, but the power of that love. My daughter was fragile. Everyone in that room with a loved one was fragile. There was sickness and sorrow, there was hope and prayer. And oh yes, there was bravery. For each of us the bravery may have manifested in different ways, but it took courage to come week after week, month after month and bear witness to the ravages of the disease, for the sick and for the well. We were the community apart from the competent medical staff. When our loved ones offered a fleeting wan smile in treatment, it gave us the strength to continue waiting and hoping for the end of the dread disease.

Sometimes there was laughter, moments of intense happiness, giggles. Carrie, when she was feeling a bit stronger, would bring her guitar, cover her bald-head with a spiky red Tina Turner wig and before her own treatment began, she'd play for the children. She'd play for all of us. No matter how compassionate the staff, and they were, her music was a break in the grimness of the hospital routine. I can still see the little children, 3 and 4 years old, walking with blood bags infusing life into their little bodies. I still hear the delight in their voices from another patient's music.

We were present as witness to the struggle for life. Within that serious medical struggle, we managed to say without words that each day lived was a day of success.

For some death came at the end of treatment. For others, life continued. Each day there was a blessing.

I can still hear a soft-spoken rabbi whose face has faded from memory. In a small synagogue, he offered a priestly benediction to an elderly man on the occasion of his 90th birthday.

May God bless you and keep you,
May God's presence shine upon you, and be gracious to you
May God's presence be with you and give you peace.

Yet the laying on of hands my mother offered me and that I offered my daughter Carrie had a calm that restored not only me but Carrie. I had little strength left after a long afternoon, hours of waiting to retrieve my daughter and drive her home. I, too, wanted to sink my body onto one of the beds in the cubicle reserved for those whose need was greater than mine.

I wondered how it was possible for her to walk. At times it was not possible. I was overwhelmed by my own fatigue. But I managed to find a wheelchair, somehow seemed to shovel Carrie in, push her to my old beige car, and drive back to her apartment. And then the thought as I drove, one eye on the heavy Los Angeles traffic and the other on her nodding head, surely eager for her own bed, for the blessing of sleep that would mitigate the effects of the chemotherapy drugs on her thin body: How would I get her down the few steps to her apartment past the fragrant eucalyptus tree and to the doorway? I was depleted, but not as much as she was. She was barely conscious. Months of treatment had taken its energy from this vibrant young woman.

I pulled into the driveway and there was Robert, her brawny young bachelor neighbor.

"Need help?"

"Yes. Would you…"

I didn't finish my sentence. He opened the car door, scooped Carrie out and into his arms and down the steps before I could say another word. He carried her into the bedroom and gently laid her down on the bed.

"Thanks, Robert," I said.

"No need, just call me. Anytime."

We stood together at the door. Awkwardly. As he walked away he muttered, "Brave people." I did hear him. The bravery was Carrie's.

I covered my eyes and recited a blessing for Robert's timely appearance and back in the bedroom quickly covered Carrie with two blankets, my old gray woolen coat, and the beige angora tam that my mother crocheted, warming Carrie's completely bald head. Satisfied that she was sound asleep, I walked out onto the patio and remembered that it was the last day of 1987. I looked to the San Gabriel Mountains silhouetted against the winter sky, and saw three flocks of birds in V-formation move across the cloud striated pink-apricot landscape.

Before sleep, I recalled a moment of levity that morning. A dark curly headed physician stuck his nose into the treatment cubicle; his stethoscope hanging from his perfectly cut blue serge jacket, glasses perched just below the bridge of his nose. He asked Laura Miller, Carrie's chemo nurse, a question about another patient.

Carrie lifted her bereted head from the pillow, "Who's that Mom?"

"Dr. Jerry Rosen, I think."

"No," Laura Miller said, "that's Dr. Hamburg."

I walked out into the corridor and caught Dr. Hamburg before he went on to his next patient. "Sorry about the name confusion."

He laughed. "It's all right. We all look alike around here. We're just Jewish boys giving chemotherapy."

The laugh was good. Remembering the interchange as I sat watching the day turn to dusk, I realized that even a small bit of humor could take the edge off a difficult day. Bold and brave physicians offering a chance at life for the seriously ill.

The caring, one for another, is what creates a sense of connection, one human being to another. The unexpected gift of caring from neighbors and friends sustained me as I watched my beautiful, dark blonde, tall daughter, usually full of smiles - become so thin, so worn -- that I could not see how she would recover. But I was certain she would. A friend arrived with a warm pair of socks, my mother crocheted that soft white angora hat for her bald head, another brought chocolates, yet another bounced into the bedroom with a brunette wig and when she settled it on her shiny head, we laughed. She looked so much like me, her mother, a brunette with brown eyes. Carrie's eyes were chameleon, green, amber, and rarely blue.

She was 31 years old and she was going to beat this cancer. And she did.

With love and prayer.

The Letter "C"

CONNECTION

Connection comes in many guises, it comes with celebrations, it comes with serving or being a member of a community; it comes with sharing. Martha Munzer comes to mind.

Martha Munzer died on September 13, 1999 just shy a week of her 100th birthday. She outlived her family, probably her early intimate friends. She created new friends, a family of friends. I met her for the first time when she entered one of my writing classes. She was in her early 90's then, tiny of stature, white hair, and always well dressed. I'd arranged my writing workshops in horseshoe fashion so we could all see one other's face as we spoke. Articulate Martha pulled her chair up closer and closer to me, almost next to me.

When I asked why, she said, "I don't hear so well these days. Do you mind?"

We introduced ourselves with some brief biographical comments. We learned, not from Martha, but from one of her friends in the group, that Martha Munzer was one of the first women, if not the first, to enter MIT (Massachusetts Institute of Technology) in Cambridge in 1922.

When asked about her sleeping arrangements, Martha was quick, "Oh, there were no facilities for young women. I was housed in a hotel."

Martha had a fast wit and charming smile. She spoke softly and we had to crane our necks, stop rustling papers to hear her. Three years later I asked the writers to write about themselves, to write a birthday page in order to facilitate a free flow of language without thought of syntax. Martha, who had written and published several books by then, questioned me, "Any page?"

"Yes, any page out of your life."

This is Martha's page:

"GOING ON 95"
By Martha E. Munzer

When one is reaching the end of the line, what is it that one has learned in these many, many years? I have a very simple formula: keep doing what you have been doing all through your life—but modify it as you go along.

Thus, instead of a daily swim of 5 laps in the pool, I've gradually changed the span to 4, 3, 2 and sometimes to 1. But I've never skipped a day, even in winter, in an unheated pool. My tough old body can take and enjoy the cold water, rain or shine, no matter what the season.

My daily hike has also been cut in size as time progresses, but the enjoyment has remained constant. So may it continue as long as it's possible.

As in the inevitable approaching death, I turn to E. M. Forster's wise words, "It is thus, if there is any rule, that we ought to die—neither as victim nor as fanatic, as the seafarer can greet with an equal eye, the deep that he is entering and the shore that he must leave."

The "deep" may actually turn out to be oblivion. One's hope is that one may live on for a while in the hearts of those whom one has loved. This is the only immortality I wish for or believe in.

I hope that when it comes time to call it a day, I shall know that I have lived and that hopefully, I have in some small measure shared my life."

This was Martha's legacy to herself and to everyone in the room. She epitomized the sense of sharing that women who connect know well.

A year later I met Martha at a baby naming. She looked beautiful, old, but lovely.

She wore an emerald green silk dress and the only adornment was a small gold pin. Her companion was a much younger man, in his late 80's, his head crowned with thick white hair that complimented his pale blue jacket.

He was annoyed with me, "How do you know Martha?" as though staking out his territory.

"She's a friend," I said.

Weeks later I met a mutual friend of ours, Rosemary.

"Have you met Martha's friend?"

"Yes, I have."

"I have something to tell you."

"Well, Martha said her friend didn't know how to do "it", so she taught him to do "it" and now they do "it".

So Martha at 96 was still doing "it". Amusing yes, but the thrill of life for Martha was there every day. It was a life savored, a life well lived and a life shared. Martha lived alive and died in peace. No matter the age, the urge to be part of life continues.

But oh, the magnificent journey. The yellow tulips on my desk. The falling petals catch my soul. Stems straight and strong; no hint of demise. Golden tulip petals, so perfect in harmony with life begin to wither and curl. Only one blossom has two petals clinging to the mother stem. The others will follow; I cannot say when. So I wait and watch and let it be as I, as we, play out our lives.

No life is perfect. Life taunts each of us, yet there are moments, sometimes days and weeks when we find some form of perfection. The stew on the stove smells delicious. An unexpected kiss from a child warms the soul.

An unexpected call from my childless friend Nancy C. in the days when I lived in Barcelona, Spain, an expatriate with two small children, would set me scurrying about the old Sarría apartment, cajoling the maid Juanita to hurry with lunch.

"Nancy is on her way!"

Juanita, fat and sweet, usually lumbered around her kitchen filling the air with the lovely aromas of her Catalan cooking, but with Nancy on the way I could hear her feet scuffling across the floor. She'd been roasting a fish akin to red snapper and I could smell the saffroned rice with which she stuffed the fish, smell the garlic most certainly glistening in the olive sautéing the slender slices of white eggplant. Juanita called out to me in Spanish, "I know, I know, all will be ready for the Señora Nancy."

There was affection in her voice. Nancy would slide into Juanita's kitchen, open the stove and nod her approval. Then surely, she'd lift the lid off the soup pot and ask, "Juana, (shortening her name) what is that magic ingredient in the soup?" And with a serious tone, Juanita would say, this time, "Ground hazel nuts." The repartee went on, the teasing delightful.

Nancy was coming. She was tall and slender, with dark blonde hair and an English horse face, so they said. She always wore ugly brown flat shoes. But to me she was beautiful. Nancy was my contact with all things American; she was my contact with the English language, someone I could speak with without worrying about my Spanish verb tenses all twisted in my mouth. I'd studied Spanish in high school; two years of "*Como está usted?*" two years of conjugating irregular verbs, two years of struggling with subjunctives that I was sure I'd never use. Wrong!

When we first met at a gathering for foreigners living in Spain, we jockeyed around one another, not quite sure of the beginning of a friendship. But we were connected by a common language and a common culture. We were Americans living abroad. Nancy introduced me to Barcelona's magnificence, to its history. And so we would walk the streets of this old vibrant city in the days of Francisco Franco's reign poking here and there, into back alleys, and always we'd stop at the cathedral in the heart of the old city. She and Al were married here. Slowly, slowly, she'd walk with me down the aisle, showing me how the guests nodded their approval, how her white bridal gown trailed down to the altar.

Nancy made certain to walk me into the adjacent 14th century cloister of the cathedral. There were and always are 13 geese in the central courtyard. Each goose represents one year in the life of the martyr Santa Eulalia.

Then we'd walk around the great Cathedral (known as La Seu) in the downtown Gothic district. Each time we entered the room with the votive offerings, I'd stop and marvel at the huge wall hung with replicas of hearts, arms, legs, and hands. They were made of some kind of creamy colored plastic. They were startling in number. I never did ask if these votive offerings were petitions to answer a prayer, or were they there in gratitude for a cure. I, at first, was horrified at these symbols of grief, perhaps symbols of thanks, dumbfounded by this need for public display. Only later did I come to feel, to understand the need for public prayer. There were no names, just anonymous body parts. There was privacy. And there was prayer: There was connection to God.

And for me there was connection to Nancy. Nancy was always there to help me out of a linguistic nightmare. One bright morning, bouncing along with my straw basket to the market place, armed with a list in Spanish, written out for me by Juanita, I bought a bouquet of pungent, yet sweet blood red carnations from the flower lady on the corner. Then bravely I stepped into the large grocery store, open completely on one side to the bustling market place. I waited my turn. Tentatively I read the first few items on the list. No sweat, I got it right.

Then I asked for "*un kilo de Judíos*".

There was silence. All the women stopped and stared. I'd wondered what I said. Then I pointed to a huge burlap sack of dried white beans on the floor behind me. The grocer smiled, nodded at my error, but did not explain what I had said. All he said was, "*Si, un kilo de judías.*"

That afternoon when Nancy arrived for lunch I repeated what I asked for at the grocers. She burst out laughing.

"My dear Ruth, you asked for a kilo of *Jews*."

"Let's have lunch. The children are waiting," I said.

I did feel stupid, but foreigners can and do make slips of the tongue.

After lunch, Nancy rose quickly from her seat at the table and said, "We're off to Montjuich."

"And why, may I ask, are we going up there?"

"We are going to this hill above the city to round out your day."

The children, down for their two- hour afternoon naps with Juanita, were safe. We could leave. Nancy had parked her small Spanish car on the street where we lived, Calle Madrazo, off the Calle Balmes. She hurried me; "We have to be at the funicular on time."

The steep ride up to the top was exhilarating. Suddenly we were there and there in front of us was this enormous stone statue of Jesus Christ and a huge cross.

"If this is a Catholic place of awe, then why is it called Montjuich?" I asked Nancy.

"I have no clue as to why, but the word, I believe, is medieval Catalan for the term Hill of the Jews."

Spain was a place of continual discovery and it was almost always Nancy who pointed the way. One language led to another and one faux pas led to another avenue to be explored. In the days of the *Francismo* (the reign of the dictator Francisco Franco) the Catalan language of northeastern Spain, in the province of Catalunya, was not tolerated openly.

A year passed and then another. Nancy and I parted. She remained in Spain.

I returned to the United States with my husband and children. We corresponded, Nancy and I, on onion-skin paper, waiting for at least six days before our letters arrived for answers to our queries, to comments on our lives apart. We were behind the day's events, behind the small talk that women engage in.

The letters, in time, became year-end greeting cards. Then there were none for months. In those months, my husband and I divorced and Nancy and Al slept in separate bedrooms in their apartment in Vallvidrera. Their marriage seemed to be dissolving as well. Telephone calls were too expensive in the 60's. So time and an ocean ended not only our daily contact, but the letters stopped as well.

David, a lawyer, and I had been dating a year after my divorce. He was planning a trip to Barcelona, Spain as a graduation gift for two his children. I asked him to find Nancy and give her my handwritten letter. David agreed. He would see Nancy when he arrived in Barcelona. Two weeks later, he returned and I met him at his apartment, anxious to hear the latest news.

"Well?" I asked. "How's Nancy?"

"Nancy is dead," David said.

"You're joking." I laughed.

"No, I'm not. Nancy had an aneurysm during a hysterectomy and died on the table."

I covered my face. The connection was broken in fact. The connection would never be broken in my memory.

We bond not only to each other, but to the printed word where we lose ourselves, where we dream secret dreams, where we choose a life path, where no one can find us, where we can just be. By the time I was five, I knew there was a world outside of me, outside of my parent's 3-room Brooklyn apartment, a world of words in a book.

By the time I was eight I discovered the word 'library' and its physical plant. By the time I left my first visit to the public library I made a vow, the vow of a hungry child. I would read every book in the library. I smile now at my naiveté, but then, I was thrilled at the very thought of words upon words, words that would rescue me from the mundane, words that would take me far, far away, at first into fairy land, into the land of make believe and then further and further into the miracle of the printed word and its capacity to connect me to the writer of these words. I was inside someone else's thoughts. Later I read books about Albert Einstein and wondered at the theory of relativity, at his quest into unified field theories; I read cookbooks, and novels and short stories and memoirs and essays by political pundits. I read and I read. I love the Irish writers, I love literature and Shakespeare and the new young minimalist writers.

If I don't like a book after 100 pages, I do put it down. But no matter, someone else will enjoy the book. So I return it to the library and find another. I read stories to stay alive. Stories connect me to the other; to the human I do not know. I am grateful for the gift of another mind on the printed page.

Today when I enter a library, there are young and old busy at the free computers, connecting them not only to local or national words, but to the entire globe. The Internet has connected us; I am sure, in ways yet unfathomable to so many who grew up in the twentieth century without escalating technology. Yet, we do still connect with words. We *do* look for story. It is the human way.

Interconnection has come of age. We connect to people we have never met, across oceans, across mountains. If we make mistakes in our language, it is of no concern; we are speaking to each other with words on the page. It is my hope that we do not lose each other to the miracle of electronic connection, to social networks like Facebook and Twitter, to smart phones and iPads, but do stay connected in human form, eye to eye, body to body.

We connect to heal our wounded parts. When hurt, we connect to ourselves. A mother kisses a boy's scraped knee, a man holds the woman who has just given birth to their child. We connect to celebrate the ordinary. We connect to celebrate the joy of daily life, however it falls upon us.

We are human.

We need one another to thrive. And so we shall.

The Letter "D"

DARING

Of all the letters to choose from, letters that would conjure up some thought, some memory, the letter 'D' was so filled with possibilities that I left it for the last writings of this book. I made notes in notebooks, on scraps of paper, in my daily diary, on my to-do lists and then finally I sat down and wrote without thought, wrote as the words came to me.

Above all, 'D' is for desires, for dreams that we give voice to when we are very young, or do not tell anyone, merely harbor that secret, that one day I shall…. *What* is that secret, that passion that *I* shall do? Some work out, some don't, so best not to tell anyone. I have no recollection of my childhood dreams except for that unquenchable desire to have Saturdays appear more often in the week.

Saturday was the day my mother walked me and my brother to the library. Ah, the library, that miracle place that promised words upon words, stories to fill the heart of a little girl. So the years passed, from elementary school, on through high school, and finally college. My life was mired in books, in academia, but somewhere there was that part of me that wanted to see the other side of the mountain, to leave the Bronx behind me, to erase the sight of five story brick buildings jammed together on street after street, filled with people, with families, living and dying. I wanted out. There was a world to see, a world to know, and perhaps a world to conquer. What I did not know, what I could not fathom, was what I would find.

When I came of age, when I finished college and married my husband, it was then that the dreams and desires took hold. It was then that I discovered the meaning of the word *daring*. A dream without the daring to follow through is lost yearning. Did I consciously know that we were daring? Did that word ever cross our conscious thought?

Never. We were young. We were immortal, as only the young can be; we could do anything, go anywhere and we did. We were the promise of tomorrow. We would live in Europe and leave the comfort of New York, the city that nurtured us into young adults. The twentieth century had seen wars of mass murder, both World War I and World War II. It was 1950, the beginning of a golden age for many, for those who lived through the War, both in Europe and the United States. Adolph Hitler and the havoc his Nazi regime wreaked were gone. The War was won. It was done.

And we were set to make our fortune, not in money, but in experiences lived.

On our first trip, the summer of 1953, we rented a scooter and scooted across the heartland of Europe from Paris to Vienna. We were determined to return the following year and

live in Europe. We went back to the States, me to my high
school teaching job, and my husband to his collection of part
time jobs. We saved enough to live on for a year, or so we
thought. When we returned to Europe, we bought a pale green
Volkswagen, a beetle. In that car was our life savings, our capital. We were certain we would find work. At the end of the
summer, on our last stop, our last hope, in Vienna, Austria
my husband found a job as a stringer for the International
News Service, and I taught English at the Austro-American
Institute for would be émigrés to Canada, the United States and
Australia. I was paid a dollar a class. It was a start.

At the Institute's employment office, I asked for tutoring
work. My husband's meager $17 per week (converted from
Austrian shillings to dollars) was barely enough to feed us and
pay for the two rooms we rented on the *Strozzigasse* in central
Vienna. A small brazier into which we fed coal to heat the
rooms during that very cold winter barely kept us warm. Yet,
Carpe diem. A Latin phrase that I'd learned my college days.
Yes. Seize the day. Be open to the 'yellow brick road'. Follow
it; let it lead you to the unknown. My tutoring brought us
into another world; smuggling for stateless Jews who survived
the industrial killings perpetrated by the Third Reich. Within
weeks of my meeting with Hanoch (a fictitious name), we sold
our Volkswagon Beetle and bought a 1950 hunter green Ford
outfitted by master Italian jewelers in Milan to serve as a professional smuggling car. It had ingenious hidden compartments for
goods bought by a group of Jewish men and women who had

survived the war. They had lived in the woods, in the sewers, in the concentration camps and sold in Spain and Italy without paying the required duty at the borders. We loaded the car with gold bullion (then $32 an ounce), in a very secret place, raw silver in rice-like pellets was poured into a special compartment, cameras and light meters into other compartments.

My husband often drove for twenty hours at a clip, stopping about five times to refuel the car, have a slug of coffee and off he drove. I kept up a steady stream of prattle to make sure he remained awake and alert. At the borders, particularly in Italy, I would get out of the car, while my husband went into the customs building with our passports. I flirted with the guards who pointedly walked around the car flicking the doors for hollow sounds, but our car was so skillfully crafted, it eluded the best of the crossing guards.

It was exciting. It was daring. It was potentially dangerous. Arrest might have been in the offing. It required the utmost discipline. And it fulfilled part of a dream to help the survivors who were young, most of them teenagers when they fled to safety; both girls and boys who then became men and women after four years of living as outcasts, now without family, without education.

It was an experience I'd never dreamed of, and it became central to our lives, both in Vienna, and in Munich where we later moved. Hanoch's operation was centered in Munich.

So we moved once again. Somehow a job at the news desk in Radio Free Europe was arranged. Perhaps Hanoch had a hand in securing the position for my husband. I will never know. A position on the news desk was great cover for professional smugglers. We were in our mid-twenties then. At least once a month we drove our *parnussa (earner),* our green 1950 Ford sedan for the loosely defined 'business' consortium of Jewish men in their late twenties, or early thirties, who had survived the War hiding in sewers, living as Christians in plain sight, living in the forests of Poland, those men who had lost everything as young teen-agers. As far as the staff with whom we became friendly, yet wary, we were touring Europe, and no one at Radio Free Europe ever knew of our other life.

When I reflect on the daring of the very young Jewish refugees who survived the War, I cannot fathom how they lived on a day-to-day basis, hiding, eating bark, stealing from farmers, strangling animals for food. They were quiet. Silent, lest they be discovered. Oh, they lived and they died. There is no one to count the numbers, but one by one by one, each with a name and a family, had committed an act of unquestionable daring. Their feats of silent bravery go unrecorded, unnamed, but they are remembered in the abstract. They were teen-agers with the physical resources to survive the brutally cold winters, the rains, the sleet, the ice, the hot summers. I knew some of them. I dared not ask about the detail of their daily lives in the forest outside Cracow. I was in their presence. That was enough. They were the survivors who lived to be witness to the lives they lived, and to the lives that were destroyed, murdered. They dared to begin again, day after day, week after week, month after month, year after year. It was decades ago, and I remember them as I remember yesterday. Clearly.

Daring takes many forms, daring is what makes progress, daring creates change.

Dare to be who you are.
Don't listen to those who say, "It can't be done."
Follow the dream.
There is much to discover.
Life.

The Letter "E"

EDUCATION

For me the primal discovery was in education, in the classroom. Those were the most exciting days of my childhood. In my home there were no books, there was no music, there was no radio. As a five year old in kindergarten I knew where to begin, where to find books with words printed on pages, words strung together that created sentences. Even the word 'sentence' was thrilling for me.

I can still see my mother's hands, small and slender, her fingers crooked to form words, words to teach me the English language, a language so difficult for her to write, a language in which she wanted desperately to be fluent, a language in which she foundered, often lost in a maze of the printed words she could not comprehend. Spoken words came at her with a speed that she could not unravel. Had the words arrived in photos, or diagrams or paintings, in images that she could see, perhaps then, she might have achieved a pictorial fluency.

But in her hands, there was a fluency that defied translation. So into that world, the world of Sign language, I began my education. Education was the word that my mother insisted was my entryway into the world of the hearing, a world where I could and would excel. As I grew into childhood and adolescence she taught me, along with my father, to be a teacher. They asked the questions, and I had to provide the answers with great clarity, in words they could comprehend. They taught me one of the enduring principles of teaching: repetition. Repeat and repeat in as many ways as possible a thought, a phrase, a concept until clearly understood. Clarity was essential. At times, people around me find my repetition irritating, but for me it is soothing.

English was the language I was to teach at the Austro-American Institute in Vienna, loosely connected with the University of Vienna, nine years after World War II crippled parts of central Europe. I was barely out of college, had a teaching degree and two years of teaching experience in the New York city public school system. The first post was at an all girls school in Harlem, the next teaching position I had was at the Manhattan School of Aviation Trades on 53rd Street off 3rd Avenue. There were approximately 3000 boys, an all male teaching staff, except for 3 women, an English teacher, a librarian and a young floating social studies teacher, me. I had a brawny male teacher assigned to me each period of the day. When I complained to the principal that I suspected different people were following me throughout the day, he explained that it would be safer if I were protected.

It was time to leave the system and go elsewhere.

My husband wanted to work for an international news ser-

vice, a foreign bureau of any large US newspaper. He'd graduated with a degree in journalism from New York University and
we were off to conquer Europe, the continent from which our
grandparents had emigrated. After many cities, many inquiries,
many rejections, we arrived in Vienna, with most of our money
invested in a car, our major cash outlay: a pale green 1953
Volkswagen. It was there that my husband found work as a
stringer for INS (International News Service) and I set up some
semblance of a home for us. I had to navigate my way around
the city, find stores that had palatable meats, affordable winter
root vegetables, and then find a job to supplement his income.
His pay was scanty, the equivalent of seventeen US dollars each
week. Barely enough to sustain us.

Certain that I would find work at the University of Vienna,
I, with great and false confidence, in my non-existent German,
asked about a teaching position in what was probably the
equivalent of the registrar's office. I was immediately referred
to another freezing cold building and a person whose name
has long floated out of memory. Oh, yes, they were pleased to
have me. Could I start the next day? The pay wasn't much, but
it was a place to anchor me to my days, and each room had
a stove filled with coal that warmed the lecture hall before I
arrived. Good.

The year was 1954 and I was delighted to have a paying
teaching job, even at the grand sum of one US dollar an hour,
or 26 Austrian schillings. Austria was cold that winter and the
money bought coal to fill the brazier and heat the two rooms

my husband and I rented on the *Strozzigasse*. It was a low rise building on a downtown street where we shared a water tap with the neighbors on our floor. We did, however, have our own bathroom. A distinct plus.

To save money, I walked each teaching day to my classes at the Institute. I had a great gray coat and shivered all the way. It mattered not how many pieces of underclothing, sweaters, scarves or gloves I wore, Vienna was cold, and I was never warm until I reached my room, greeted my large class and put my backside as close as I could to the warm coal stove at the front of the room. Those who sat in the front rows removed their coats, those to the back of the room, huddled into them.

My students were all adults, all older than me, and all eager to improve their English so they could immigrate to Canada, the United States or Australia. Their eagerness to speak clear, correct, precise English was evident. They were engineers, dentists, housewives, doctors, working men and women who had a connection to someone in the country they wished to flee to and they all had a working knowledge of English. Good spoken English would be as important to them as their passports and visas. So it was with serious intent that I prepared each lecture for each class. They looked to me for colloquialisms, for accent correction and for fluency. When I listened to their German speech patterns, I fathomed ways to introduce them to English sounds rather than German ones. And I often thought of how my mother struggled with the imitation of sound she never heard. Not once in her lifetime.

The lecture hall broke into smaller groups for pronunciation practice. I played music for my students. They loved Frank Sinatra.

In one of the smaller classes, I noted one of the young women who never spoke but picked at her eyebrows, plucking the hairs out with her fingernails. Her fingernails were bitten to the quick. She sat week after week, never missing a class and never uttering a word, except to respond to her name, Clara G. when I checked attendance. She sat in the same seat, directly in front of me, closest to the stove. Her eyes seemed glued to my face. At moments I was uncomfortable.

She was a slight woman, one might say 'non-descript', but when I played music for the class, she'd tilt her head and I'd hoped to see a flicker of a smile. Sometimes she nodded her head in what seemed to be approval of my teaching or of the music. She was always the last to leave the class; she'd linger at my desk as I gathered up my papers, put on my coat, readying myself to leave the room. Once in the early days she said as she walked with me down the hall to the staircase, "Good evening", in a small voice. I was about to speak when she sped away from me, down the stairs and I could not wish her a 'good evening' in return. She puzzled me. Often, as I prepared dinner, in our cold apartment with old gloves on, the fingertips cut off so I could slice and dice, cook and rinse, I'd think about Clara and wonder why she invaded my consciousness. There was a connection. I'd have to wait for her to come to me.

Clara was clean and neat. She wore the same gray wool skirt

and a different blouse, but the same dark green sweater to each class. As the weeks became months, Clara offered a faint smile when she slid into her seat. But she still did not participate in the lecture hall or smaller conversation classes.

Then one day, almost at the end of the teaching semester, when I knew everyone by name, when I was comfortable with their language patterns as they spoke English, I said that after I listened to a simulated conversation in English between the dentist and the engineer, "Your accents in English are so similar to the Yiddish accents I heard on the New York streets as I was growing up."

No one spoke.

Then, a male voice from the back of the lecture hall shouted, "How dare you compare us to those Jews!"

There was a consenting murmur in the room. For the moment I was frightened. But the war was over and Vienna was an occupied city: the Russians, the French, the British and the Americans each had a rotation in governing the city and the country. I held my breath and thought it best to let the moment pass.

I was 23 years old.

The class would be over soon. I gathered my things as I did at the end of each class, anxious to leave, and this time Clara spoke to me. "I will go with you to the streetcar."

Her face was calm, her hands at her sides. We walked slowly, side by side until we reached the corner away from the Institute. She faced me and said, "I am Jewish. You are Jewish. Never tell them you are a Jew."

"How do you know that I am Jewish?"

"I feel, yes?"

"Yes."

And in those four words a friendship was born.

After each class, we'd stop at a café, not too close to the University, and we'd talk, always with an admonition from Clara, "Be careful of your words in a public house."

I hadn't given Clara's age much thought. I would have guessed her at 40 or so. She was 28 years old, the sole survivor of her family, the only one who left Auschwitz alive. She wore long sleeves every time we met. I didn't ask, but I did wonder which numbers she had stamped on her arm. I asked for her address, and her reply was immediate, "Oh, I live in a room with a widow. I change my room often."

When the semester was over we met for the last time at yet another café. She always wanted to go somewhere where she had not been before. We sat inside drinking hot coffee with whipped cream floating on top, aware that we would probably never see each other again. I looked at her face, her soft brown hair, the woolen cap she pulled off her head and put on the table, hoping I would not forget her soft eyes, her rare smile. Clara opened her coat, slid her green woolen sweater away from her blouse and removed a silver filigree pin with the words Rachel and Jacob inscribed in Hebrew and said, "This is for you."

I protested. "I cannot accept this."

"I have no family. I have no one who will remember me when I am dead. You must take this and remember me."

I never saw Clara again. She too, was my teacher, the first to educate me in the importance of remembering not only the past, but the people who entered my life and then left, leaving me with yet another facet of life lived. She taught me the meaning of patience, the understanding of waiting *until,* and I understood that there was no "until'. Now was the future.

For her and so few others out of the six million Jews industrially murdered, survival was not only by one's wits, but by random chance. She had no family and she chose me as a surrogate. I was and am deeply honored. Clara taught me the importance of family, the root of the past.

I wear the pin still.

The Letter "F"

FAMILY

My family is the bedrock of my life.

And if I am to write about my family, I have to return to the beginnings of the women who touched my life: My grandmothers. They are like all grandmothers, known and unknown, who touch the females who come after them, sometimes in memory, sometimes in stories handed down, sometimes in faded sepia photographs, and certainly in the genetic imprint on their bodies, on our bodies. Their stories become our stories, the repeated threads of their lives impact our lives.

I knew one grandmother, the other died before I was born. She died three months before my mother and father were married in May of 1927. I can reconstruct the life of Fanny Milkovsky Bromberg from bits of information my mother told me. I can reconstruct her life from the SS Philadelphia's manifest in July of 1908 when she set sail from Southampton, England to join my grandfather, Abraham Bromberg.

I can reconstruct her life in my writer's imagination. I am tied to my grandmother Fanny by my conjuring of her life, not as a girl, but as a young bride in the small town of Smargon,

Poland that no longer has an imprint on a current map of the area. The existing literature of the small Jewish towns, called *shtetls,* describe lives lived in small orbits, lives too often bludgeoned by Cossacks who rode through the towns brandishing whips, killing and raping Jewish women in their way, lives that often sought a way out of the brutality.

So began the exodus from the shtetls to the New World, to that Golden America that awaited them across the Atlantic Ocean. Jews sought relief from the rampant anti-Semitism of the late 19th and early 20th centuries in Eastern Europe.

The journey was hard for young Fanny. Her son Nathan was born in 1905 when she was 18 years old. After his birth, my grandfather left for New York via London, England to 'make a new life.' She remained in Smargon at her parent's small home. Fanny waited for her husband Abraham to send money for a boat ticket. Two years passed.

Abraham sent enough for the first part of Fanny and the young boy Nathan's journey to London, by cart over muddy roads, by train, and finally by boat across the English Channel. There she met her husband Abraham who found a room for them with an old Jewish family in White Chapel. What their reunion was like with 2-year-old Nathan clinging at his mother's long skirts, I can only surmise with pleasure.

Fanny was beautiful: hair long, shiny and black and eyes of deep blue. Tiny. Almost five feet tall. But her life was a life without enough money. Through my own growing up years, I had seen my mother's hands repeatedly tell me of the marvel of her mother's hands in the kitchen, how she cooked delectable food without a written recipe.

So I conjure up once more how Fanny found a way to support herself and her son while waiting for Abraham's letter. Fanny Milkovsky Bromberg, an excellent cook, baked cakes, pies and cookies for her London neighbors. She didn't charge much, no one had much. She baked a cake for Nathan's birthday and a neighbor offered her money to bake a cake for her child's birthday. With the extra money she bought enough butter, enough flour, and enough sugar to bake two cakes and then three and four and five. In time she became the neighborhood baker, baking in the apartment owner's kitchen, which she shared with 2 other families. She did this all during her pregnancy. Before my mother was born she'd saved enough to buy her own ticket. After my mother, Miriam Shifra was born, she waited for 3 months, said goodbye to the Rosenberg family, then embarked on her journey aboard the SS Philadelphia. For Fanny, this was another beginning.

My grandfather found an apartment in Williamsburg, Brooklyn for Fanny, Nathan and the infant girl, Miriam, my mother, born profoundly deaf. That discovery would come later. Fanny lived for another nineteen years and bore five more children, three more sons, and two daughters. Diphtheria ended the life of two-year-old Anna. Two of the four surviving children were also profoundly deaf. An unknown genetic history robbed them of sound. Abraham worked on and off as a carpenter, house builder and in 1939, he died of lung cancer when I was ten years old. He was a heavy smoker; his hands were stained with nicotine. I remember him and his smile, his red mustache and his gentleness with my mother.

Shortly after Fanny died, Abraham married a widow, Bertha with children, and had more children, Irene. This wife would be left behind as well. And so it was.

Whenever my mother spoke of her mother Fanny, it was to regale me with stories of her kindness, of her generosity, of sharing with others when she had so little. And when I came from home from school, and excitedly told my mother, Miriam, about my new friend, the first question she signed to me was the same, throughout the years from first grade to my graduation from college. She signed with deliberation, "Is your friend kind?"

My paternal grandmother's name was Lizzie, not that her Russian mother Rachel would have named her so. Not in a small Russian village, not in a Jewish community. Her name must have been Leah, named for the biblical Jacob's first wife, not the wife Rachel for whom Jacob labored 7 years.

I calculate that Lizzie, my paternal grandmother, was born in 1883. She died in December of 1941 at the age of 58. So it has been said. Exact ages of the immigrant population were guessed at, surmised by Ellis Island officers, by teachers, by rabbis or by a relative that had preceded them to the new Golden Land. Names were changed at random by border guards, names too difficult to write, to say. What was her name? Was her name her identity?

"To steal a name is a sin." My grandmother Lizzie said to me when I was eight years old.

I wanted to know why the theft of a name was a sin.

Before she died she said, "When you were a little girl you kept asking why stealing a name is a sin and I had no answer for you, except to tell you that is so."

That was to end my curiosity, but she too died before I was old enough to know the essence of her soul.

There was no holiday to mark Lizzie's death. I remember my father, hat slouched over his head, head bent in sorrow for the woman who bore him, walking to the subway one dismal December night, to catch the train at Grand Central station to Philadelphia so he would be in town for his mother's morning funeral, for the woman he had not the capacity to know fully. He was deaf, she was hearing.

There are no records of Lizzie's birth, no records of her marriage to Moshe (Morris) Sidransky. Her legacy consists now of her dead sons and daughters, of her living grand children, some who are connected, one to the other, others who have been lost to the geography of this vast land. But the flesh of her flesh resides within all her descendants, all the children who never knew about the double helix, who never understood the meaning of DNA, the genetic miracle of this age.

Lizzie was of another era. She married when she was 11, some said. Others said she was 13. She claimed she was 15. She was young when she married the widower Morris Sidransky, father of two children. Dora was eight then and Bernard was older. If I have the names straight. I remember Dora. She looked like an American Indian with long wild black hair and a deep voice. Dora taught me the Lord's Prayer, the *now I lay me down to sleep prayer* that terrified me lest God would wrest my soul as I slept. The memory fades. To grasp the voice of someone surely long dead (she'd be more that 100 years old) is an act of pulling shards of time into consciousness.

How did 13-year-old Lizzie fare with her eight year old step-daughter? How did Benny, my 38 year old father face the burial ground of his beloved mother? I ask for answers and I can only conjure the past as I imagine it.

But I do not imagine Lizzie, wrapped in winter sweaters, and woolen gloves cut off at her 10 fingertips, shifting from foot to foot in the snow as she stood beside her Lower East side pushcart selling buttons and thimbles, needles and elastic by the yard during the hard, hard years of the Great Depression. I see her clearly, reaching into her apron pocket and saying, "Ruthie, a penny for candy. Don't tell the other children."

I was the oldest girl, the treasure of my grandmother's life, the hearing daughter of her deaf son. There were three male cousins: overweight, wonderful Henry Warshaw, he was older than me by one year. His handsome brother Lester, younger than me by one year. These were the sons of my father's sister: Anna Sidransky Warshaw. And there was Bobby Glorsky, son of my father's younger sister, Rosie and her husband Isidore. Later there were other cousins, but these boys were the ones I grew up with.

I remember my grandmother and wonder at her life, wonder at her marriage to Morris, a man who grew old when I was a young child, a man who spent his days sitting in a musty store filled with second hand goods. He was tall and lean, white hair sparse, cheeks sunken. He was old at seventy. Dementia perhaps? Perhaps he was older than 70, but to me, as a small child, he was one of the ancients, someone to avoid. I cannot hear the sound of his voice. Did I ever register his sound? I can only smell the dust of his corner store, somewhere in Williamsburg, Brooklyn, bulging with old wooden furniture, lumpy mattresses, blankets and sheets, pillows and pillow cases, worn clothing, a violin hanging from the ceiling, and wooden milk boxes stacked high in one corner filled with corks for wine bottles, children's toys, and a pair of roller skates that he ceremoniously gave me with a smile and a touch of his withering hand on my five year old arm one summer's day. It was my birthday. This was the act of kindness I remember. So I named my son, Mark, in honor of my paternal grandfather. His Hebrew name is Moshe, for Moses.

Had my grandfather, Morris paid for the discarded furniture, or was it furniture he salvaged from the streets? I have a vague memory of young families huddled beside their possessions piled on the street. Strong men, out of work, who could not pay the rent. And so they were evicted with all they owned.

My father said, "There is no work for a man. Maybe a man can sell apples on a street corner. Maybe a woman can wash floors for a rich lady. A man must feed his family."

Then, I did not understand the import of my father's sorrow.

My grandfather Morris owned the brownstone building in which we lived. 100 South Eighth Street. He'd bought it in the post World War I heady days of the 1920s, when flappers danced, and liquor flowed and his cork factory made him a rich man. An amendment to the U. S. constitution ended his small financial empire. The Temperance movement legally forestalled the sale of liquor. Prohibition was the law of the land. And Moshe Sidransky was relegated to his small dark store and his packets of buttons and thread, and second hand merchandise he bought with his bits of coin from the dispossessed. Then, one coin could feed an entire family.

There were days when families of four and six slept in the hallway of 100 South Eighth Street, Brooklyn. My grandmother, my Lizzie, had invited them for the night and had given them pillows and blankets and the use of our toilets. Was it then that she decided to buy a pushcart and sell my grandfather's wares on the street with the other vendors struggling to earn money? People did not discard worn clothing: a shirt without a button, panties with stretched elastic, a good woolen sweater worn at the elbows, a ripped hem, knickers that were too small for a growing son. Clothing was mended, not a scrap of fabric wasted, not a piece of wool from an old coat thrown out. Everything owned, new or worn, had great value.

Lizzie was in the mending business. Her customers were poor, poorer than she was. She was in the market place selling my grandfather's wares to a needy clientele. Her business was in pennies, pennies that fed her family of sons and daughters. Pennies that fed Benny and Anna, Rosie, Bessie and Sylvia, Frieda and Irving. They're all dead now. But it was Lizzie who kept them safe, at home in their own beds.

It was Lizzie I remember, praying for rain so she and her pushcart stayed at home. She could soak her feet in a pail of warm water and Epsom salts. Her feet were swollen in summer and red with cold in winter. I don't believe she set up shop on the Sabbath. Certainly, she pushed her pushcart out on Sundays. And she always smelled of the beef suet in which she fried food for her family. When the smell was strong, I gagged and fled from her side saying, "Grandma, I have to use the bathroom."

She answered me, I suppose, in English. I knew nothing of Yiddish. Did she speak Russian? So many unanswered questions. We spoke in Sign language at home. Oral English, for me, as a child, was a foreign tongue. My fluency lay in my hands. Sounds were difficult to decipher. Spoken words were a code to be broken.

I don't hear her voice. I see only the letters she wrote me in Yiddish script when my mother and father, my brother and I moved to the Bronx, away from her prying eyes. So my mother said. I missed my Grandmother Lizzie; I missed the sound of oral speech. It didn't matter if I didn't understand every word those around me said, words in Yiddish and Russian and words in English.

It was all language, and it was Lizzie who gave me words

every night. She climbed the stairs to our apartment, asking for me, checking to see if I was alive. She never trusted my deaf beautiful mother, never trusted this 21-year-old to care for me as an infant, as a toddler, as a little girl. Lizzie never knew it was I who gave my mother my own corrupt version of language. I pretended I understood everything that was said, that I was all knowing. But Lizzie, afraid for my safety, made sure that once a day a hearing person entered our apartment. I loved Lizzie even if she did smell of suet. Or was she too tired after standing on her feet all day in the sun, in the cold, in the drizzle, in the light snow, to bathe? Perhaps.

Did she fear my mother? Was it her own story that made her wary? A thirteen-year-old stepmother had a challenge. Her father sued in court to prevent his daughter Lizzie Katz from marrying my grandfather Moshe. (Morris was his anglicized name). Lizzie lied and said she was 15 years old, old enough to marry, old enough to know her own mind. The year was 1896, if my calculations are correct. Her parents were Rachel and Moshe Katz; they left New York and moved to Winnipeg, Canada, where many of our family still live. I don't know if Lizzie, my grandmother was born in the United States, or if she was part of the enormous family that emigrated from Russia.

Lizzie was among the youngest daughters of her family. Once again, records were never kept; dates were skewed, birthdays passed without note. When I checked the family tree sent to me by an Israeli cousin in 1983, Lizzie's year of birth is not listed. There are many more children, fourteen in all that I never met, but I knew they existed, born to Moshe and Rachel Katz. They are: Sidney, Raymond, Irving, Lionel, Elvin, Marcia, Irma, Annie, Clara, Lizzie, Ida, Pauline and <u>Molly</u>. They were born at the end of the 19th century and into the beginning years of the 20th century. As family lore tells, the family migrated from Russia, to Texas, to New York, and finally to Winnipeg, Canada. Their last names at birth were and probably still are Katz, except for the women who married and assumed their husband's names. And therein lies the difficulty in finding everyone.

Lizzie never saw her father again. After he died, she traveled to Winnipeg to see her mother and her sisters and brothers. She took her youngest son, Irving, with her. There are photos somewhere in a carton, in a closet of that meeting.

Lizzie was the breadwinner; Lizzie was the grandmother who had little time for me. Lizzie Sidransky's struggle was the struggle to keep her family fed and clothed, and she started with a pushcart on the Lower East Side of Manhattan. At the outbreak of WWII in Europe, my grandmother moved to Philadelphia, and opened a corner store on Arch Street, selling the same goods she sold on her pushcart. She added cheap cologne, razor blades, soaps loaded into bins for her customers. But the mainstays were her buttons and thimbles and huge spools of elastic.

I spent part of my 15th summer there. It was 1944. My grandma Lizzie was dead. Family lore says she died of uremic poisoning. She was 58, so it was believed. Her daughter, my Aunt Frieda, ran the store, and I occasionally helped at the cash register. It was in the back of that store that I was kissed for the first time by a tall curly haired young stock boy whose name was Marty. That's all I remember of the boy, but I remember Lizzie. I see her face, prematurely lined with work and worry; I feel her hands on my face and hear her murmur words of endearment. I loved her.

More than seventy years have passed and I can still sense her being, her care for her family and her terrible cooking laced with suet, animal fat that clogged the arteries of her children and led to premature death for some of them.

My children inherited Lizzie's drive and Lizzie's love. My oldest granddaughter, Rachel, five generations down the line, indirectly bears the fruit of her labors. She studied at Trinity College in Dublin for part of the summer of 2004. Lizzie, Rachel's great-great grandmother would have been proud of her. She was proud of me, proud of my ability to speak, to take care of her son Benny, my father. When I was a child in the late 1930s and early 1940s, she wrote me letters in Yiddish. Somehow I managed to read them, and write back, always with the help of a neighbor who was fluent in the language. And always there was a wrinkled dollar bill in the envelope. A huge amount of money then. Lizzie, in her way was a wondrous woman, a terrible housekeeper, a foul cook, but a warm-hearted human being who had a smile for me each evening when she returned to the brownstone building in Williamsburg, Brooklyn on the corner of South 8th Street that we shared.

How did she manage to cook for seven children, herself and her husband each night, after haggling with customers on her feet all day? She died young, worn with work. It was the winter of 1941. I was 12.

Whether it is nurture or nature, whether genetic or learned, there are, I believe family traits that are handed down, from generation to generation, grandmother to grandmother, from girl to girl, from woman to woman: perseverance, love, loyalty, courage, commitment, caring, safety. The list is endless. Traits, small or large, recognized or unrecognized, are encased in our beings; they belong to us. They are our gifts from the past.

The Letter "G"

GRACE

The letter "G" has many words to complement a woman's life, a sense of goodness, a flirtation with the goals in one's life. But for me, the word *"grace"* resonates strongly. I had to search through my journals to find the entry I wrote aboard Air Canada's flight 911 to Toronto, Canada, where I once lived.

Airborne, my mind is totally free.

I think from time to time, the thought I had as a young girl, as a divorced woman, that my best asset was my mind, my brain power—the facility to engage in great leaps of intuition, great leaps of understanding of complex data, great leaps into passionate, thrilling absorption of art, great leaps into concepts of the human psyche. And all of these leaps took place without consciousness. It was there! Simply there. A God given gift. It is the magic of life; it is the content of my life, now the writer, perhaps later another path to be taken. I think the artist, yes, the artist in my soul shall always succeed, always dominate.

To create art is to live in a 'state of grace'.

One speaks of grace. What is this grace that seizes the soul, this grace that has physical substance in the center of my chest, where that gentle squeezing occurs and I ask, "Is it my heart?" or is it that space expressed in physical tension saying you are ready, ready to enter that state permitting a free flow of thought and language, allowing human perception to hit the printed page as quickly as my pen will slide across the page (I did write everything in longhand before committing it to the computer), almost automatic writing, for at that moment, there is no thought, no concentration, there is flow, much as a young river runs through a deeply cut mountain The flow is unstoppable; the movement of hand and pen no longer governed by my conscious will, but rather as witness, as writer, as one who paints the landscape in broad strokes, in broad outline, no impediment. The movement is smooth; the relationship of artist to craft, of artist to soul is One. Perhaps at some level it is in direct relation to that ancient Hebrew prayer, the Shema. Perhaps the unity of soul and act puts one in a divine state, a state of 'grace'. Perhaps 'grace' is Jewish in concept, but goes by yet another name: a mitzvah is a command to Act. If the action is taken within the unity of soul — the union of act and spirit, then perhaps art is work that is created in a 'state of grace', in that divine space where holiness and action are one. One.

These thoughts assail my conscious mind. Twenty, thirty, forty years ago when I was occupied solely with women's tasks, when

I craved thought, when I asked the question regarding 'art', I was aware that practicing art would create the 'whole', not in the psychobabble terminology of finding oneself or establishing one's self esteem, no, not that, but the total human being connected to life's purpose. I do believe that each life has purpose, each life is important, each life touches another, each life gives to another, in whatever form.

This is the 'state of grace', the gift of life, not in the sense of a total life, to give a small or large gift to another, to touch the other. Some do it as famous people of science and letters, as entertainers, or politicians, or clergy, others do it by living, what some would see as small lives, lived within a narrow band, seemingly mundane lives as did my parents. But I have given the gift of love they gave me to others, to a large audience, in a book.

And so it is.

One life touches another.

One life illuminates the other.

Perhaps in that frame, I can approach my writing life, my work. The phrase, "hope is triumphant' rings of platitude, but the illustration of that hope is the triumph of art. The gift of story telling enhances another, entrances the soul, fills the reader, the listener with awe. And Awe is reserved for the Mighty, for God.

So each touching must be, in some way related to a higher purpose—to a 'state of grace'."

Grace arrives without warning. It is the moment of the

unexpected smile, of a stranger waving me on as I approach a street corner in my car. There is gratitude in grace. A time received with unspoken, at times, unknowing awe. They were the moments of nursing my children after they were born and understanding the cry of hunger. It was the nod of approval from the bullfight fans in Barcelona as I nursed my son delicately covered by my ecru linen shawl.

It was the deaf blind woman with whom I could sign words directly into her sensitive hand and see the pleasure of comprehension on her elderly face.

When I entered a room where Helen Gribbs sat, she immediately signed, "Ruth is here."

Did she smell me, did she sense my walk; did she *know* the response of others to my entry? Whenever I saw Helen the only way I greeted her was to throw my full body weight against her body so she could feel me. She could not hear me, nor could she see me. But *I* could see her face light with a broad smile. That was always a moment of grace. Always her first question was signed openly, her face filled with glee, "How are you Ruth?" It was not the commonplace salutation. Patiently, I'd sign either my joy or my woe of the day into her feeling fingers. She'd nod her head and offer me words of consolation or words of delight. I could not fool her. She had a highly developed sense, intuition, one might say, that could detect any false statement. Perhaps it is a gift given only to the multiply handicapped. But I dared not use the word 'handicapped' in her presence. Helen was complete unto herself.

At the High Holy Days service for the deaf, her friend Julius signed for her, keeping her abreast, as best he could to the prayers in English. When the *shofar* (a ram's hollow horn) was sounded heralding in the Jewish New Year, Helen beamed and signed, "Beautiful music." She never heard a sound in her entire life. Musical melody was transmitted through her feet, through Julius interpretation into her hand of the signs of the interpreter on the *bima.* Julius was deaf. As a boy Julius and my father Benny attended the same Manhattan school for the "hard of hearing". When Julius hugged me hello, it was a touching of my father, dead so many years.

Grace is a fleeting chance encounter. One January night as my husband and I dined at a restaurant, a wind blown elderly man and his wife were seated at the next table. I guessed him to be about 90 years old. His wife and I shared the same banquette, our purses abutted. If they were connected, perhaps we were as well. I liked the man immediately when I saw him. He smiled at me as he sat down; I smiled back. My husband gave me ' the look' that said, -- *Don't start a conversation.* -- Inwardly I knew that as soon as I could, I would chat with him. But first I listened, in truth eavesdropped, on his talk back and forth with his wife. They shared a fish dinner, he had blackened mahi-mahi and she stuffed shrimp. She offered him a shrimp and he said, "If it won't be taking anything away from you?"

She speared him a shrimp on her knife and passed it across the table and nodded her head as if they did this frequently. She was dressed for dinner out, in a black outfit, and he was casual, a blue sweater over his shirt.

I turned to my dinner plate and picked at the food, much more interested in the two people beside me. When he said to his wife, "I had fun writing the short story this afternoon and I finished it", I thought *another writer*. I must talk to him. I did speak with him, and he was delighted to engage in conversation. "I am Sid and this is my wife Phyllis." His wife was shy but he went forth like a warrior, telling me about his part in a local condominium theater production.

He asked, "Will you come to see me in the play?"

"Yes, of course."

We exchanged phone numbers and I knew we would never contact one another again. Yet, it too, was a moment of grace.

Grace is everywhere, in the smallest acts of life. A woman nursing her baby is surely in a state of grace. Kissing someone you love, a child, a mate, a parent, a friend, a pet is all part of the grace of life granted. Making love with a partner is an essential element of grace. A walk in the park, a sense of nature's forces, the birth of springtime, the lushness of summer and the fall harvest puts me into a state of grace. It is amazing that so many of the ordinary moments of life place us in grace's path. Is grace an element of happiness? Perhaps. Grace is a state of being for me, a place without words, a place given to me spontaneously. It is there when I least expect to be flooded with a sense of peace.

The Letter "H"

HAPPINESS

Hope is a daffodil. Daffodils come up yellow every spring. That is my sentence, my mantra, when life puts up a roadblock, when I struggle between hope and despair. When in the month of October, my daughter was ill with lymphoma, I promised her that the daffodils would come up again in the spring and she would live to see them, not only that spring, but for all the spring times in her life. These days, when the month of March is announced on the calendar, she calls me and says, "Mom, I have a bunch of yellow daffodils on my table," I say an internal prayer of thanks.

Every day is a day of hope.

Healing old wounds, particularly emotional ones that cling to the psyche, can be a difficult journey to maneuver, at times seemingly impossible. Deep wounds engendered by family members one to another are hard to heal, but there are ways and techniques to begin the end of strife and find the path to harmony.

I had a dream about two loaves of *challah,* the braided bread prepared for the Friday night Sabbath, for the welcoming of the

Sabbath bride. We bless God for the bounty of the bread we are about to receive, and so the *challah* is made for breaking bread with those we love and care for.

I dreamed the dream on a Friday morning and by 7 AM (my writing hour) I had written most of it out in longhand, rushing to remember the pieces elusive to memory. I awakened with shards:

I'm in a strange town looking up at re-gentrified old, old buildings. In a large city, surely. Barcelona, where I once lived, perhaps? Near water, a river, a canal, the Mediterranean Sea, an ocean. I'm not certain. I'm with someone. My daughter? We're in an open-air market, redolent of harvest peaches and pears. There on the corner is a bakery, and through the window I can see through to the back shelves filled with loaves and loaves of freshly baked challah. The open door and the aroma of warm yeast pull us into the small brightly lit shop. We buy bread. My daughter and I each carry a well-baked whole challah slipped into a clear plastic bag sealed with a red tie into the crowed street.

Dilemma. We have nowhere to put the challahs until the evening Shabbat meal.

Why do we have no place? The question looms, 'Where can we place two loaves of bread?'

I say, "I shall ask someone on the street for a place."

"No, you can't do that."

She looks into my eyes. It is Carrie my daughter with long golden hair.

"I shall ask someone with a kind face," I say.

A middle-aged couple passes by me. She carries a full bag of groceries. I don't see her face. She is well dressed. He seems involved in their conversation. They must live in a nearby building.

I interrupt them and ask, "May I store these challahs with you until this evening."

"Yes, "she says. "I live here."

The building bricks have a pink tone. Sunlight shines through the brick pores.

"It's a three floor walk up. Do you mind?"

"No, of course not." I say grateful for her offer.

I carry both loaves. I find the climb difficult, I breathe heavily, clutching the two plastic bags of bread. The stairwell is narrow and dark, not black, just dark, unlit and windowless. It winds back and forth like a mountain road. The banister is polished mahogany. There are two apartments on each floor. I am surprised when I walk into the bright spacious apartment and see her husband already seated on the sofa with a young woman, a daughter I suppose. My daughter is not with me.

This nameless, kind woman without facial detail leads me to the large window to see the view, and then to the refrigerator. She opens the door; the cold air hits my face. The shelves are filled with green liter sized bottles. Wine?

Water? There is little food, only tidbits to tickle the palette, cocktail teasers, olives in small jars, unopened and placed evenly on the middle shelf. I raise my arms in an attempt to hand her the two loaves of challah.

I awaken.

I know this is a dream to hold. What does it mean? An epiphany?

The loaves are healing symbols of family members who are toxic, one to the other. Is this my interpretation of maladaptive behavior of people? Is healing possible?

I hold the sacred Sabbath bread. The strange woman is the third party, the arbitration counselor. I try to make sense of family estrangements. The dream is a clear indication of my wish to heal a family breach. Instead of an olive branch, there are two loaves of challah, a bringing together of people. Perhaps a family can once more break bread and end all misunderstandings. Not all breaches end happily. Then I say blue pencil these people out of one's life. Be gone.

There can be healing in trying. If the attempt fails, there are healings to be nurtured in endings. For every ending, there is a beginning, a clean slate. It may take time but to begin again is another measure of healing, another path on that ever elusive path of happiness.

Although my mother Mary has been gone for many years, I can still see her hands comforting me, signing the words, "You will be better. You must honor yourself." These were her words when I told her of my husband's betrayal with yet another woman and the final end of our marriage. How rare to hear the word *honor* spoken and how often I saw the word *honor* fall from my mother's hands. She formed the letter 'h' with both hands, raised them to each side of her forehead, head bowed slightly and extended her hands outward fractionally. The word *honor* so said in Sign. It is a beautiful expression of the word that she took seriously and taught me to consider in every relationship I formed from childhood into adulthood. To see the exact syntax of her sentences on the printed page might be jarring to the eye trained in reading fluid prose, but the prose in her hands was incisive. She was about to erase my pain of abandonment, albeit momentarily. She signed, "Come, we'll find your father, he will make life better."

So we found Benny, my father, in the next room entertaining my young son and daughter. His apparent purpose on this earth was to make everyone who crossed his path smile. He too was profoundly deaf, left so by meningitis when he was two years old. He never heard Bobby McFerrin sing his 'don't worry, be happy' song, but Benny made us happy with laughter. He motioned the children to watch his marvelous feat more than once. And on this day he performed it once again. He positioned himself against the bedroom wall, turned to the children and said, "Look at me carefully."

Certain of everyone's rapt attention, he moved quickly into a headstand, his legs straight and his feet high on the wall. Then, slowly, he moved one hand to his mouth, removed his false teeth and clacked them on the floor. Of course, he couldn't hear the children's glee at this silliness, but I knew he knew. I, too, was moved to a broad smile. Down he came in one swift motion, teeth still in his left hand and with a swoop, he slid them into his mouth. On his feet, the children ran to him and he scooped them up in his arms and when he put them down after the hugs and giggles, he signed, "All happy now?"

I had his gift. He gave it to me unwittingly. It is the gift of happiness, and knowing how to reach for it in a sad or bewildering moment.

Play, laugh, smile.

(Grandpa Ben did a head stand when he was 67 against the brick wall on our patio in the small town of Columbus, Indiana, when he and May visited with us. We have a photograph of it !)

The Letter "I"

ME

The letter "I" begs to talk about me…the "I" that inhabits my body and soul. But I reach across my thoughts to Albert Einstein and I quote, "Imagination is more important than knowledge." Therein lies the thrust that keeps humanity striving for the next and the next great invention, the next idea that will shake the world and change the way we think and conduct life. One scientist builds on the shoulders of another, one artist, be it in music, theater, painting or writing, seizes the moment of understanding, the moment of the intuitive leap -- that unknowable, unnamable knowing -- that creates human expression, to go further and further, vaulting us into yet another sphere.

The world as we live in it today would bear no recognition to the world of my grandmothers and how they lived their daily lives, riding by horse and buggy, standing behind a pushcart selling wares people today would ignore. Their thimbles and thread would be of little use to today's consumers who throw out the barely worn and buy new.

These grandmothers formed the basis of my pursuit of life

in all its facets. They were women of enormous strength, and when their strength could no longer support their burden, they died. May their memory be for blessing. They taught the I *of me* how to live in ways that I will never be able to enumerate. I stand on their shoulders.

I have a lock of white hair that people stare at from time to time. They ask me the name of the salon that did such a great job. I often answer in a flip manner and say, "Oh God put in that streak. Or maybe it was a gift from my Grandmothers." The response from the curious person is generally a snicker. Once when I was shopping in the supermarket, a little boy, perhaps 6 or 7 years old with outrageous red hair asked, "Lady, can I touch that?" I bent down and he gingerly stroked my white streak.

Dr. Petrus Johannes Waardenburg, a Dutch ophthalmologist, studying deafness in Holland, *intuited*, that the frontal white streaks in some people's hair was genetically related to deafness. He gathered this thought without any specific concrete data at hand, except for years of observation, supporting his assumption. He reached that hunch, his own intuitive leap, after he saw white cats killed on highways. He intuited that these cats were deaf. Further research showed it was true. His discovery was intertwined with imagination, experience and intuition.

Women are gifted with intuition it seems, in far greater numbers than men. Mothers hear a baby cry, and by the sound of the cry, can usually tell the mother what the baby needs. Why women have uncanny intuition, I cannot say. It is often referred to as a 'gut feeling'. How often have we heard the expression, 'trust your gut."

It is my imagination that compels me to sit down with a blank book, (yes, I still do most of my writing in longhand) and excavate the markers of my life. Why? To preserve my days and upon rereading an old journal find out who the *I of me* is. Perhaps, in part. Quite often, I am astonished by the words I wrote twenty and thirty years ago. Have I discovered the *I of me?* No, I have not. Instead, I have come to the realization that life is a process and I am governed by the unfolding of the day, each day different.

We lead busy lives, perhaps too busy to listen to our own imaginations, our own intuitive leaps. We need time out, time off. There is a Spanish saying that delights me: *It is good to do nothing, and rest afterwards.* I love that sentence; it makes me chuckle. Really? Rest? Do nothing? How then shall we achieve whatever newness is out there? My mother, illiterate, yet so bright, often prodded me to sit and think. Thinking, she cajoled, would create new ideas, a new way to cook a chicken, an accidental word to prick a fleeting thought, and I was to write all my thoughts down in a notebook. I was to write them down, so I would not lose the idea. I was to be a writer. Maybe, she hinted, I would write a book and tell all her stories one day. I did do that, but not all her stories.

There are too many to tell. I, like most women in the Western world, share common rites of passage: we are born, we are educated, we marry, we have children, we are divorced, we are widowed and we continue on alone. Some do, some don't. Abruptly life's journey ends, sometimes with warning, sometimes without.

I try to intuit the meaning of life with my imagination. I fail. What is the question that plumbs the meaning of this day, of that day, of my life, of your life? Of anyone's life? Is it to serve God, or to serve the powers that be, or to serve ourselves? There are calamities and joy, and blessedly there are ordinary days when we rise to the day with pleasure, when nothing untoward happens, when we are not greeted by war, or illness or injury, financial crisis, flood or storm, or the death of a loved one.

Just an ordinary day when I go about my business, when I do the laundry or the shopping or stop to chat with a neighbor about the good weather we're having. I do not ask, what or why, as my children did when they were three and four years old, because I did not have the answers then and I do not have them now. I remember a conversation that my daughter Carrie and I had when she was three years old. She wanted to know where rain came from. I said the rain is in the clouds and when they open, rain spills out. She looked at me wide-eyed and said, "Why doesn't the cloud wear diapers?" So much for the imagination of the very young. It is delightful. Do we, as adults, allow our minds to roam into unmarked journeys?

I can only search memory. My life was packed into each decade of my life, and each decade was another challenge, another beginning. Without conscious awareness, I was learning how to live, storing experiences, chronicling my life and my times into my psyche for reflection when I no longer had the need to race headlong into life's fortune, good or bad, or ordinary. I have thousands of pages of words, all words I have written, always as witness, into bound journals, onto scraps of paper that I have saved, and into daily diaries, all in a scrawl that I sometimes cannot read. I do not have much time, even now, in my eighties, for reflection. I am busy beginning again and again. To begin and begin again is the secret to unravel. "Follow the yellow brick road", take it where it leads you. Let your imagination fly. The story of Genesis is the story of beginning and then beginning again.

So I began an unexpected chapter in my life in Barcelona, a period that I now see as part of the "I" of me. My son was three and my daughter was six years old. All of it was random chance.

I was asked to be the founding director of the American School of Barcelona. The school was designed for Spanish children whose parents wanted them to be fluent in English.

Flattered, I said, "Of course."

All I had to work with was a building, in a residential section of the city; the building, a beautiful old home, was the first in Europe to house an underground bomb shelter, built by the Loyalists, the faction that opposed the dictator Francisco Franco. I was told that this mansion was the headquarters of Juan Negrin, once Prime Minister. I didn't question whether or not I had the capacity to organize this alone. I knew I could.

Using imagination and intuition, I modeled the structure of the school after the New York City school system. I was trained there. I ordered textbooks, hired teachers, and the school was opened to students from nursery school to high school seniors. I had ideas, I was innovative, inspired by the challenge. I was confident and I was exhausted. The year was 1962.

Later I learned that I had the distinction of hiring the first rabbi to be on the staff of a secular school, or any school, in Spain since the Spanish Inquisition. He was a French rabbi whose name has been erased by time. He visited the school and the few Jewish students once a month. A small marker, a large marker.

Behind my office desk, hanging on the wall, were photographs of John F. Kennedy, Francisco Franco and Jesus Christ. How strange it must have been for the handsome rabbi to be interviewed, by me, an American Jewish school director, Kennedy, Franco and Christ all facing him as we spoke in my poor French and his impeccable French.

I also hired a Baptist minister to speak with the Protestant children. These were the children of Americans who worked for large companies in Spain.

The last religious leader I hired was a priest, my beloved Father Arimon, who looked after the prostitutes on the Ramblas. Prostitution was legal. How he came to be interviewed I don't remember, but our connection was immediate. His smile was wide; his love for the children immediate. He'd arrive at the school in his cassock and wide brimmed hat every week, wisps of white hair struggling for space on his wide forehead, looking for me, checking up to see if I was all right, if the Spanish way had not completely floored me. It did not floor me. In my apparent arrogance, (I was not arrogant, merely overwhelmed by the task of setting up an organization without notes or guidance from anyone, two children at home, a household to run, and an errant husband) yet I forged ahead with lists upon lists on long sheets of paper, hoping I would be able to read my jottings, my reminders of things to be done.

I had no doubt I could run a school. My mother instilled enormous confidence in me as I was growing up. I was her magic child, I could hear, and could tackle anything, be anything. I was the classic parentified child. I was the leader and anything asked of me I could and would do. All I had to do was step in, claim my inner resources and the task was done. Or so I believed, and in some measure still believe, although age is upon me now.

In that process I discovered a part of the *I of me*. I understood then that there are many parts of me, as there are many parts of all of us: this revelation did floor me. I understood that acceptance of all the parts of me, known and unknown, then and now, now and future are the *I of me*. My intuition was clearly at play.

I didn't have to imagine the rest of my life, just let it happen. My imagination would carry me.

So it was. And so it is.

The Letter "J"

JOURNEY

The word *journey* enters my consciousness. As I near the last years of my own journey, I peruse old journals, old photographs, and realize that there are names and faces that have gone completely from memory. I know these faces, these places, these people are all part of my journey. It is not essential I remember every detail of my life, but that I accept that every detail is all part of my life and will continue to be part of it until the end, until my last breath.

Digging into my past is meandering through hand-written bound journals that began seriously multiplying in my adult years. They were written in different places, from Europe, to North Africa, to Canada, the United States and in different decades of the Twentieth Century. Now, I continue into the Twenty-First Century. Pack rat that I am, I've saved letters, not all of them, and some are breathtaking to read again, a letter from my grandmother Lizzie Katz Sidransky who wrote me when I was a child, letters from my ex-husband pleading with me to return to our marriage after his lengthy affair with his skinny secretary, some letters from my children at camp in their early handwriting. These form the journey's memory. Each of us has our own unique memory of time past, and hopes for the future for however long, from beginning to end.

The *journey* is a series of beginnings for most people, certainly for most women. We begin again and again, and the journals are for me, a testament to the journey I have taken. The journey is both internal and external. All that I have written in my lifetime is part of that journey, published and unpublished. Writing somehow makes my journey permanent, indelible, something for me to hold onto as time ends, something for my family to know me by in generations to come.

There is a Chinese proverb that says, and I paraphrase, *if one keeps a record of one's life, one gets to live twice.* Lovely thought, for some parts of life, not for others.

The *journey* takes place within and without, but always in context, in a society, in a place, in a house, in a room, on a street. I like days without specific plans so that the mystery of the day will unfold, will open for me as a bud into leaf on a tree. I am most always dancing within my own thoughts, my own linguistic symphony. And like my mother, I am continually amazed at the day's wonder. She enjoyed the day with her eyes, pointing out a lone monarch butterfly in the spring, noting the first steps of a human on the snow's landscape and often with the words she signed, "Look at everything. You will learn the world."

These were not her exact words, but certainly they were her intent.

There are journeys of childhood, of the young, the middle aged and the old. Each journey stamps its mark on each human being. At times, we remember significant moments, at other times, moments of hilarity or shock, sometimes fear, and these are moments that stay with us.

On the first journey away from the United States, Saul, my husband, and I rode a Vespa across Europe, from Paris to Vienna. We were young and strong of body and spirit. We were not sophisticated. The trip was long and we were weary at the end of the fifth day of travel. We reached Vienna at nightfall, late. We didn't know where to stay. The city was dark, locked up; there was no one on the streets. Saul sat straddled on the scooter and asked me to go into what appeared to be a luxury hotel and ask for a room. I walked across the barely lit street, the *Ringstrasse*, and walked into the revolving door and into a Russian soldier who pointed his rifle squarely in my face. He said one word, "Nyet!" I never stopped moving through the revolving door until I was once more on the street, striding quickly to the Vespa. "No deal, the Russians occupy the hotel."

"Get back on; we'll cruise around until we find something."

A taxi driver pulled up beside us as Saul revved the motor.

"Wait," I shouted. "I'll ask."

In fractured Yiddish, (the closest I could come to German) and in English, I asked the cab driver to recommend a hotel. He said, as far as I could make out, in German, "Follow me!" We followed him around the unknown streets and when he slowed down, he pointed to a small hotel on the corner of the street and then quickly drove off. The desk clerk asked questions in German. Our German was non-existent at the time. He shook his head and gave us two sheets, two pillowcases, a blanket and a room key. "Zimmer drei." Room 3. The number was on the key ring. The bathroom was at the end of the hall. Exhausted, we quickly made the bed and fell asleep, only to be disturbed throughout the night with the sounds of doors closing and opening. Early the next morning I made my way down the hall to the bathroom. A pleasant, buxom, blonde opened the door, nodded, and said, "Guten Morgen."

I asked tentatively, "Do you speak English!"

"A little."

"What does, 'am stunde o die nacht' mean?" My German was not accurate.

She snickered a smile and said, "By the hour or the night."

I rushed back to my sleeping husband and said, "We're in a whore house."

We lived in Vienna for a year after that. We later searched the streets for that hotel and never found it again.

The journey is about process. How do we succeed with life from one day to the next, how do we function, how do we respond to moments of great joy, how do we cope with difficult days, with tragedies that befall us all? There is truth to the cliché that 'no one escapes' life's unforeseen bumps in the road. Some have heavier burdens than others, yet they too manage to find joy, if not at the difficult moment, then later. For me, the words *joy* and *journey* are somehow inextricably twined together. They resonate with life's passage.

Of all the journeys I have taken, the most joyous have been the birth of my children. Today, when so many women are delaying childbirth for a career and too many are unable to conceive, there is confusion about the reproductive role of women. The confusion relates to the word *when*. When shall I begin having children? is the question so often asked, the question that begs an answer when a woman in her forties asks her doctor, "Am I too late?" The answer most probably is 'yes,' unless the woman is willing to undergo a battery of choices that were unheard of fifty years ago. I do understand Dr. J's, (a Florida gynecologist) comment that women have little use after their childbearing years. I can only assume that he was far too harsh in his judgment of women's roles.

The journey of motherhood in years past was never a question of timing. You entered marriage soon after your teen years, and as soon as you were able, you had your first child. The days of my grandmothers – one had as few as seven children and some as many as sixteen -- are long over. Large families are a rarity today, but it does not dispel the joy of having fewer children, or even one child. To feel life within your own body is a miracle. I can think of no other word to describe the intensity of pleasure I felt when my daughter, in utero, kicked me. Alive, alive this baby of mine. All part of life's process. We live, we give birth, we die. Simple, yet complex.

My children are part of my journey, as I am part of theirs.

Love and laughter were part of that journey and continue to be so and continues on to their children, my grandchildren. My task as a mother was to teach my children whatever I knew, whatever I could in any way I could. I would not deny them the negativity they would find, but I grounded them in the meaning of love by example, by affection, by telling them daily I loved them, telling them sincerely, by story telling.

When I was a child, there was no television. My images were in my imagination and my imagination was fueled by my love of fairy tales. One of my favorite stories was of three princesses who were commanded by their Father the King to describe their love for him. His plan was clear; he would call them in one at a time and listen to each one's declaration of love. The answers would decide who would inherit the kingdom upon his death. The youngest princess was his favorite. The two oldest daughters plotted to share the kingdom and each would tell their father that their love was grounded in precious stone. The eldest daughter was called in. She knelt before her father and said, "I love you more than all the diamonds and rubies, and sapphires and emeralds in the world."

The King was pleased.

The second daughter knelt before her father, the King, and said, "My father, I love you more than all the metals in the world, more than all the gold and silver that can ever be mined."

The King was pleased.

But it was the youngest and fairest daughter he wished to

hear, for it was she that he wanted to be the Queen of the Land. Days went by before she would appear before the King. She kept putting it off. She had to think of an appropriate answer. On the day she finally went before the King, she wore a beautiful white dress, a simple garland of white flowers in her hair, and knelt as the other two did before her father and said, "Father, I love you as much as meat loves salt."

Silence.

The King was struck dumb. When he spoke he said, "You do not love me at all! You are hereby banished from the castle." With that pronouncement, he called to his guards and ordered them to take her to the forest to live in a cabin for the rest of her natural life. She was not to set one foot in the castle for eternity.

Weeping, she was led away.

A year later, a handsome prince out riding in the forest saw the young princess drawing water from a well. He fell in love with her at once, and sought her hand in marriage. After weeks of proposals the young princess agreed. The prince brought her to his castle and arranged for their wedding within the month. He asked his lovely bride-to- be if she had any requests regarding the wedding banquet.

"Yes," she replied, "I wish to be in charge of the kitchen. I wish to instruct the cooks in their preparation of the food and invite the neighboring king and his family to the wedding celebration."

The wedding was lavish, the food sumptuous. As the young bride instructed the cooks, the meat had *no* salt. She watched as her father, the king, who did not recognize his daughter, taste the meat and spit it out.

He shouted, "The meat is putrid! It has no salt! I came all this way! I have lost my daughter and traveled so far for putrid meat!"

This time, he wept for his lost daughter. The young princess then declared herself, and, as in most fairy tales, the King was jubilant and they all lived happily ever after.

Love comes in many guises. Recognizing the myriad forms of love takes listening, really listening to the intent of the words of others and more importantly to the actions of others. Love is substantive. Love is inclusive, not exclusive. Love of family, love of children, falling in love all have a common denominator. For each of us, the intimacy of love is singular, unique, be it the love of a mate, of a parent, of a child, or of a friend. All different loves, yet all somehow the same.

The journey is a solo flight.

Then the question arises, "What is the meaning of life?" What is the purpose of the journey? I've asked the question, and I've had many answers, none of them, definitive, at least for me. Yet, they are provocative. When I asked a Hassidic rabbi to explain the purpose of life's journey, his answer was quick. "We live to serve God, and we serve God by serving others." The simplicity of the answer begs the complexity of the response. It requires digging, thoughtful contemplation, which brought me to several words. One stands out: Compassion. Caring for the other, whomsoever that other or others may be, is the meaning of life.

When I asked my cousin Andy B, half in seriousness and half in jest, he, too, was quick with his answer. "The meaning of life is another question. "What's for supper?" Think of all the ramifications of that simple quip. Of course, we work for our food, gather it, buy it, prepare it, sit down to eat with family or friends. It's all there. Food is essential for life, and the steps necessary to bring food to table is all about connection, not only to the farmer, to the cattlemen, but to the earth itself. It is the earth that feeds us, that binds us to life, to our journey. The journey is not about independence, that much touted word, but to the word, *interdependence*. I hold the *journey in awe*.

Each person during his or her lifetime will face both small and great difficulties. Physical and emotional pain does enter into our psyches. For some there is financial hardship. For others the death of a loved one colors our waking hours. For some it is a wedding day. We share life's vagaries. We are human and subject to trials during our time on earth. I find comfort in the words of Psalm 30:

> Weeping endureth for the night
> Joy cometh in the morning

The Letter "K"

KINDNESS

My life in the recognition of kindness and the giving of kindness began with my mother, in the 1930's, when I was a little girl, growing up, searching for friends, not quite sure of myself, wondering if I could ever make one. After all, what does a five year old know about those with whom she comes in contact? Very little. I have flashes of strong memory. One in particular is of my mother standing in front of me, watching as I drank my milk and ate my slice of rye bread and butter when I came home from school ravenous with hunger.

"Well," she signed, "did you make a friend today?"

I nodded my mouth full of bread. Then she signed, "Is your friend kind? Very important to have kind friends."

I asked her to explain her sign for 'kindness'.

She reached over and touched my head. "You will know soon who is kind and who is not." That was the enigma with which she left me. My mother, although functionally illiterate, was emotionally intelligent with a keenness not given to those of us blessed with all our senses.

To this very day, when I am introduced to someone new, I

look for kindness in the flecks of their eyes, in their hands, in their smiles, calculating quickly if the smile offered is genuine. All this takes place, most probably, within a nanosecond. If I'm comfortable with what my mother taught me to see; she never heard the sound of the human voice or its subtle nuances; I offer my own smile. But a smile is not necessarily a kindness. Yet, I have come to trust, for the most part, those who smile at me in return for mine.

When my son Mark was five years old, I left him in the care of his paternal grandfather at a playground in Queens, while I raced across town in a taxi to visit my 8 year old daughter who had just undergone a tonsillectomy in a Manhattan hospital. Then I raced back again quickly to relieve my ex-father-in-law. He held the apparently sleeping boy in his arms. As soon as he saw me, this tall older man, walked quickly to my side. "It's nothing. Mark fell off the swing and banged his head. He'll be fine in a few minutes."

"How long has he been asleep?"

"About twenty minutes."

Alarmed, I slipped my son from his grandfather's arms and went quickly up to my apartment. I called the doctor. He said, "Grab a pillow, get a cab and take him to LIJ hospital at once. Make sure they X-Ray him."

As quickly as I could, I followed his instructions, hailed a cab and never looked at the driver, calling my son by his name over and over again. No response. His eyes were shut tight.

At the hospital I reached for my purse to pay the driver. No purse. I'd left it on the hall table in my rush to get to the elevator and onto the street.

"Please give me your name and your company, I promise to send you a check as soon as I get home," I said to the cab driver.

"It's ok lady." He opened his door and then opened mine, helping me out with my unconscious son Mark. He walked to the hospital emergency room door and although it swung open automatically, he waited for me to go in. I barely looked at his face and I didn't answer him when he said, "Good luck lady."

I ran with Mark in my arms into the emergency room. Within minutes he was gone, whisked away on a gurney by an orderly with a nurse in quick pursuit. I waited, and I waited, and waited. Hours passed. A young resident asked for me. He said, "It might be a skull fracture. We're not quite sure. You can stay, but I know you have been here for hours. Go home and get some sleep. I suggest you come back in the morning."

"Will he live?"

"Go home and get some rest. We'll have more information in the morning. We'll take good care of your son. Go easy." Numb, I walked out the doors of the emergency room onto the steps, into the dark night. I'd forgotten that I had no means of transportation home, and no purse, no money.

I stood there immobile, not quite knowing where to go. Suddenly a yellow cab pulled up in front of me as I was about to step down into the parking lot.

"Lady, here I am. Get in. I'll take you home."

It was the unnamed cab driver. He'd waited for me.

I slipped into the back seat and in silence he drove me home to my Queens apartment building.

"Lady, we're here now."

"Please wait. I'll run upstairs and get your money."

I was alert, looked for his name and his cab number. I checked the back of his head, his neck was strong, his hair thick and black and his name had an Italian cadence. I'd be sure to send him money if he drove away. But he was too quick for me.

"Lady, forget it. It's on the house."

He drove away.

Mark did not have a skull fracture; it was a concussion. In the morning I made certain that I had my purse with me, cash and my checkbook, and hoped that I would hail the same cab. I never saw him again. I don't remember his name. But I do remember the kindness. Days later I told my mother the story of the cabdriver while we sat in the same park. I signed and she signed and we talked, always keeping our eyes focused on the children at play. She made a single clear sign, *kind,* a circling of her middle finger in the center of her chest, close to her heart.

Years after the incident with Mark and the cab driver, my father Benny died and my mother moved to Florida to be near me. Aging has its perils and my mother did fall and break her hip. It fell to me to be sure that she went out, particularly to the beach to be close to the ocean she loved.

We sat together staring at the October ocean. I heard the slap of water on the shoreline, the shouts of children, the roar of people sitting on the beach. She did not. The silence was good;

speech was superfluous in the Florida sun. We were sheltered from it directly: a large wooden canopy shaded the deck at the bottom of Palmetto Park Road.

The gazebo was open to the public and there was no one on the benches except for me and my mother. My mother's wheel chair was in the trunk of my car. The distance was not great from the parking space to gazebo, and she managed the small rise with her walker. That pleased me. She sat on the bench closest to the railing. She touched me, a cue to pay attention to her words. My mother lifted her hand and pointed to an outrageous bikini, smiling at the firm buttocks completely outside the scant navy blue covering. Tired of sitting, I rose and rested my elbow on the weathered gray wooden railing, turning my back to the sea. I faced my mother and we began our conversation in earnest, she commenting on the beach scene below us. She moved her eyes across the sand catching meaning in movement, at times ignoring my rapid fire responses to her signed words. I raised my head from my speaking hands as an older couple passed between my mother and me. The man moved haltingly behind his wife in single file, following her step for step. His right arm hung limp, his fingers curled into his hand.

Stroke, he'd had a stroke. I focused on her spiked dyed blonde hair and was taken momentarily aback when she softly asked, "Is it all right if we sit here at the corner of this bench?"

I nodded yes, a bit annoyed. There was ample space away from us. Why so close? Yet I said nothing. The gazebo was open to the public.

The woman said to her husband, "Here darling, drink this, I am so thirsty. You must be thirsty too."

Wordlessly he clutched the paper cup filled with Lemon Crush and sucked up the sugary ice. He slurped.

My mother said, "Why aren't you paying attention to me? What are they saying? Anything important?"

"Nothing!" I signed.

I ignored the couple so close to us and resumed chatting with my mother, all in Sign. I felt the eyes staring at me, at my mother. Growing up in a deaf household I was used to people turning their heads to look at us, some stared for a moment or two, some were embarrassed and turned their heads quickly. Not this couple. Finally annoyed at the brazen staring I turned to face them and said, "Fascinating, isn't it?"

Undaunted, the woman said, "We tried to learn. We went to classes to learn Sign language, but it was too complicated for us. He gave up and we gave up."

I cocked my head waiting for her to continue. "You see my husband can hear, but he can't speak. He had a stroke a year and a half ago. The therapist taught us the alphabet so that my husband could spell words to me. That way he could tell me what he wanted. It was too hard for him to form the letters for each word. "

My mother, anxious to be included in the conversation, waved her hand in the air claiming recognition. I felt a subtle shift in the airflow around me. I moved my face close to my mother's and told her the simple words that had been uttered.

Her language, American Sign Language, once maligned, and now a legal language, accepted in high schools and colleges for serious study, was a key to opening a communication door for Leon, a stranger.

The woman interrupted my hands, "Is that your mother? You have the same face, the same bones. You are both beautiful."

I was ashamed of my rude tone.

My mother ignored the woman and signed, "He has one good hand. You teach him some sign words. Forget the alphabet. Stupid therapist. What do they understand of people without speech?"

It was a command.

I walked over to the man and said, "Would you like to learn Sign, a few words perhaps?"

He shouted at me, "Kay, kay, kay" before I could finish my sentence.

I clenched my fist and put my thumb up in the air. "That is the Sign for the word 'good'."

He raised his left arm; his right was useless at his side, and awkwardly attempted to sign the word 'good'. I leaned over him, so closely that I pushed his golf cap off to one side of his head, took his hand in mine and formed the word 'good' for him with his own hand. He was pleased. His eyes spoke anxious for another word. The word 'bad' came to mind, and I took his hand in mine once again and created the Sign for him. He had trouble folding his fingers over his palm and raising his pinky to sign the word. Within seconds of practice, his hand in mine and then watching my hand alone, he was able to form the word on his own. I didn't remember that the sign I taught him for 'bad' was a home sign and not universally accepted. But never mind, he wouldn't know, and now it was part of his new vocabulary.

"Now when someone asks you how you feel, just give them a sign."

His eyes filled with pleasure. He smiled a crooked, but a happy smile.

"Would you like the word for 'happy'?"

"Kay, kay, kay," came the immediate response.

I splayed my fingers apart and gently patted my chest, thumping it rhythmically. He caught on at once and thumped his own chest, grinning at me.

His wife, silent during the brief lesson, stared at me, uncomprehending. I avoided her eyes, uncomfortable with her unblinking stare, and instead spoke to her lavender and white checked shirt. "He can learn anything. And as long as he can use his left arm and you understand the sign, you can be his interpreter."

"How can we do this? It is so difficult."

"There are people here in Florida that can help. They can teach him and they can teach you. It will end his frustration and yours to a very large degree."

"Can you teach us?"

"I could from time to time, but I'm so busy these days. I know people who can do this." I gave her my card and asked, "What is your name, your husband's name?"

"I am Frieda C, and this is my husband Leon."

"I am Ruth and this is my mother Mary." I simultaneously signed and spoke the introduction for my mother. She was on her feet, supported by her metal walker. With her left hand, she was left- handed, she pointed to her chest and said vocally, "I am Mary."

We all smiled.

Leon, excited, signed his three words and asked, "Kay, kay, kay?"

"Leon, shall I teach you more Signs?

His eyes answered, "Yes".

I taught him the signs for 'yes' and 'no'. He was quick now.

"There are other signs you might like to have right away." I pinched my fingers together and put them to my mouth." This is the sign for the word 'eat'. He created the sign with his fingers like a young deaf child might and burst into tears; his creased face turned hemangeoma purple.

I kissed his cheek and his raging emotion subsided.

"Another sign Leon? Are you ready?"

"Kay, kay!" He said strongly.

"Let's practice. Do the sign for 'yes'. He confused 'no' for 'yes'.

I repeated the sign again and again, knowing well that repetition is the key to learning. He grasped the difference.

Concerned about his wife, I asked her, "Frieda, where are you from?"

"We're from Brooklyn, New York, but just before Leon's

stroke, he retired and we moved here to Florida. We live close to the beach."

I fixed my eyes on Leon's and asked, "What did *you* do in Brooklyn?"

Frieda answered, "He was a Manhattan lawyer. He practiced general law."

I signed this for my mother, interpreting for the spoken voice.

Frieda's voice quavered as she continued, "What shall we do? I want him to learn to speak again."

"Find a good and understanding therapist, one who knows Sign. He can have speech therapy and learn Sign at the same time. It is the way profoundly deaf children are taught."

My mother interrupted calling my name Ruth in her soft voice, "Ask Leon where he went to Law School?"

"Leon went to St. John's in Brooklyn."

His voice broke in, "Kay, kay", and his right hand signed the word 'yes'.

My mother showed Leon her fluent sign for the word 'yes'. Leon mimicked her sign accurately and she applauded his effort. She signed, "Tell Leon, I know where St. John is and it is a good school for lawyers."

I told him what she said and his eyes smiled at me. I talked to him alone, touching his shoulder, limbering his good hand, stroking it, putting the sense of language into his arm and hand. We continued for another hour and the teaching was rapid, the words came quickly: sleep, toilet, hungry, cat, stupid. I did not attempt to re-teach him the alphabet. I didn't believe he was ready to spell out his sentences. Words for now were enough. Simple words, necessary words, sufficed.

Human touch eased his way back to some form of speech, albeit in his one normal hand.

It was four o'clock, the afternoon light softened and I had to drive my mother home.

"Leon and Frieda, I have to drive my mother out west, and then east again to my house. "Call me. I'll do what I can to help."

"Kay, kay, kay, kay," Leon spat out the words in delight and signed the word for 'happy' again and again.

My mother was not allowed to sign to me as I drove, but at every red light she had a sentence ready for me. The one I remember is, "Ruth, today is a perfect one."

I never heard from Frieda or Leon again.

The Letter "L"

LISTEN

The letter "L" says listen. Listen to what? To language. My listening began with looking at speaking hands. Sign language was my first introduction to the land of words. Gifted with both hearing and the capacity to Sign my words, I, perhaps, have developed a special relationship with the verb 'to listen'. Listening to the other is paramount to connecting one with the other. Listening is essential to our humanity. Our words, no matter how we express them, convey a form of touching. We are exchanging thoughts, commands, conversation, concepts, love, laughter, humor. All of it and more, much more. We can face talk, space talk, gesticulate with our hands and arms, blink our eyes, turn away, and orally make sounds. These actions require another form of listening. It demands acuity, a nuance of comprehension. Some may call it sensitivity. No matter. It is listening with our other senses; it is a complete awareness of the movement of the other. It is knowledge of the body. Sometimes listening involves smelling or touching the other. Of all the skills we learn, listening to the other is probably the most difficult. Total listening is the most difficult *and* the most powerful.

Listening to what? What do I remember of my first contact with language? I have often asked myself what were my first impressions of the spoken word. What was the moment that I understood that a sound from a mouth made a word rather than a gesture of hand? When did I understand that a string of words created a human necklace, that the necklaces were laid side by side on sound waves that ballooned into paragraphs of the mind, touching me, connecting me to the other speaking human, connecting me to an idea or thought? Discovering the meaning of a new word continues to thrill me, even now, particularly in a foreign language, say Spanish, or German, or French, languages I continue to labor at learning.

Immediate comprehension of other languages has somehow, for me, a mystical quality. When I speak in another language I am amazed at the capacity of my brain to switch, to think and speak in another idiom. My tongue moves in unusual muscular patterns: 'h' is aspirated, 'r' is rolled, sounds emit in new ways for my mouth. Thoughts are never phrased in quite the same way as they are in English or in Sign language. It is nonetheless language; it is touch.

Sounds enter my brain, perceiving, accepting, denying, and responding to communication initiated by sound. There is music in language; each word is a litany of humanity. Each sound in each language has its own pattern, its own universality. Sounds may reinforce or belie the eye message, the body expression, the tilt of the hand, the twist of the waist; it is all a pivot of human intercourse.

Language is multi-faceted: It is the listening that is crucial.

My father listened with his eyes. If he were still alive he might have smiled his beaming smile, spreading light not only on me, but spilling it into the room or anyone else in his presence. This sensitive deaf man, cut off from language, had language in his eyes, in his hands. He, gifted with nuance, with perception beyond the norm, guarded his insights and chose laughter instead—an antidote to separation from the sounds of spoken language which he never comprehended. He would mimic a blathering mouth, and with his right hand imitate a rapid fire of words issuing from a mouth, any mouth, his hand opening and closing into a circle, look at me and with a twinkle above his mustached face sign three words, "Talk too much." I would return his smile.

"Tell me," he would say, "Tell me a story." And there it was, his longing to be part of a world from which he was ever separated!

He longed for story. He longed for life's literature. He wanted to know; to know what there was to know.

"I not stupid man, very smart, just have shut ear."

There was magnificence in his language. Short. Real. And oh how he listened!

Language is story. The story of everyman is laid out from end to end, from continent to continent. It is the story of the world and it is told in the language of the land, over and over, every day. For my father language laced the hands of anyone who would 'tell' him something of value, something funny, something to gasp at, something to simply enjoy. I learned the listening lessons at my father's powerful hands. It was thrilling to share his love of language. Language is listening. Listening is learning. Listening is loving.

Years later, after I was all grown up, the family celebrated Carrie's son Benjamin (named for my father Benny) Nes Bar Mitzvah on Ocean Avenue in Santa Monica. So many people who were part of their lives were there to join in the merriment. Among the guests was Dr. Philomena Innocente McAndrews, the oncologist who saved Carrie's life in the late 1980's.

I said as soon as I saw her, "You saved her life."

"You did it."

"No, you did it!" I said.

Philomena shook her head, her long black hair swishing on her lovely shoulders, denying my assertion. I smiled and said, "We did it!"

She shook her beautiful head once more and grinned at me.

During that difficult time, I watched Dr. Phil, as some call her, listen to Carrie, listen to other patients and connect with parents of the very ill. She too had listening skills to impart. But one had to listen.

After Carrie's first chemotherapy treatment she asked to drive my car home. I hesitated. I heard her will to be normal. She drove. I dug my fingernails into the seat cushion. She was fine.

Sometimes Carrie carried her guitar to the chemotherapy floor. She played for the children, and to see their faces as they listened was breathtaking. These were very ill little ones, yet the musical interlude removed them from their cancer fight.

In the ensuing months, I listened for the language of the ill. Carrie never complained, never said, "Why me?" She was still. There was the sense of a quiet fight against the disease that invaded her thinning frail body. We had to get through the weeks and months of chemotherapy and radiation. I listened to her eyes and watched them imperceptibly tire and I'd say, wherever we were, with whomever we were with, "It's time to go." She fought this visual listening. In time she understood that I 'got' the difference in the timbre of her fading voice, her eyelids dropping fractionally with fatigue and she'd respond with, "Okay, Mom, let's go."

At times I had to instruct those who would visit Carrie not to come, or to leave when she needed rest. Often I was greeted with their inability to hear, to listen and to respond appropriately. "Oh, but it is me, she'll want to see me." My response was a quick and immediate "No. Please listen to my words, hear what I say." Chagrined with their own conceit, they gently bade me farewell and left, usually with grace.

I learned to listen to the seriously ill with my eyes. I learned to grasp the meaning of the subtlest movement. I learned the meaning of silence. I learned that listening demands silence, not chatter. Silence was my mantle for the skill of listening. The response and my words would come later.

I was taught to consciously listen. I was taught to suck in the words of others, so I could impart them and their meaning to my parents, particularly to my father who hungered for language. I was, at the age of 9 and 10, his dictionary. I didn't know the meaning of adult conversation, but I was quick, trained in the art of listening, and when I told my father what was said, he asked, "Do you understand?"

Not always, but I repeated the words and my sense of the talk back and forth to my father. He would smile and then I asked, "What does it mean?" He shook his head. Obviously this conversation was not appropriate for a young girl. Years later, I marveled at his capacity to interpret the confluence of words that I did not understand. He taught me that listening is many fold. Listening is attention to the other. Listening, truly hearing what someone is saying, is connective tissue, one human to another. I was always amused by my father, signing to me, cupping his hand to his ear and asking me to listen to his words. They were all hand words, words sculpted in the air. Somehow he knew that he was tweaking my sense of humor with his antic posturing. Hand over his ear indeed.

When my daughter recovered from lymphoma, I returned home after almost a year of being at her side. Months later, I returned for a visit. She told me about the mangy cat that showed up at her Silver Lake, Los Angeles apartment. She said that the cat had been badly abused and would go to no one but her. She asked me not to be offended if Sam, the cat, would not come to me. I am not particularly fond of cats so I was quietly pleased that the cat would stay away. As soon as I sat on the couch in Carrie's living room, Sam jumped on my lap and purred. Carrie expressed surprise. I did not. I said, "We probably have the same smells. Who knows Sam may be responding to something similar in the timber of our voices. They calculate human beings from their perspective."

Animals listen with a keen ear.

We had a dog during the years we lived in Munich, Germany, during the smuggling years, our weekend lives, camouflaged by my husband's work as an editor at the news desk in Radio Free Europe. He was a brindle boxer, with a black muzzle usually covered in heavy drool. I loved that dog, and because I fed him stewed horsemeat and white rice, I suppose I can claim that he was my dog, although it was my husband that wanted a dog. His full name was Ariel von Festspiel. We called him Alex. There are many Alex stories, but the one that delights me is the one when we were living back in the United States, on Park Avenue, in the Chevy Chase section of Maryland. He was trained at a special school in Munich; he did graduate, but I might add, not with honors. He was a guard dog, trained with a gun, a dog that was taught to knock an intruder to the ground, and hold him there with his paws, his muzzle over the perpetrator. He had keen hearing.

I was alone one night in the house; my husband said he was away on assignment. All was quiet. Carrie was a toddler, safe and asleep in her crib. I had removed Alex's collar so he could move about freely. He was trained to sleep during the day, and patrol during the night. He never barked, but this night was different. He barked and barked and finally I could no longer ignore him. He perched on the windowsill, and barked in the direction of the one car garage.

Well, I thought, call the police. I was in the neighborhood of the nation's capitol.

When two burly six-foot men in ten gallon hats arrived at the front door, with their hands on their holsters, their guns at the ready, Alex attacked, and knocked one to the ground. It took a few minutes to find his collar and leash, and drag him off. I gave the policeman a washcloth to wipe the drool off his face. I kept my laugh smothered.

"Lady," he said, "you don't need us!"

"So sorry, he was trained as a guard dog in Germany and there is someone out in the backyard. If I give the command, *Pass auf,* he will find anyone or anything that is there."

"Go ahead lady. I'll follow with my flashlight."

And there he was, a man urinating against the garage wall.

The police retrieved the drunk but left his car in my driveway. I recognized him. He was a Congressman who evidently had a bit much to drink and lost his way. At dawn, I heard his car, saw him slip behind the wheel and drive off. He was easy to recognize.

At times, I would see him at the local supermarket or in the neighborhood, and I'd smile, and say his name. He looked at me without recognition, but as the consummate politician he nodded hello. And I had my morning chuckle.

My hearing is not as keen as a dog's but I was raised to listen, a skill that is essential in today's world of technological media, so often without human contact, denying immediate connection, eye to eye, ear to ear. Inflection of one's voice contains meaning that one does not glimmer from the printed screen.

Deaf children with cochlear implants have to learn to listen. It is not an easily acquired skill. The speaker puts his hand over his mouth and speaks clearly and young children have to learn a skill that most of us are born with. I have seen these children and I can only marvel at their excitement when a spoken word conveys meaning. Their faces light up. What joy! There is joy in listening.

The power of listening, however that listening is achieved, is a gift sometimes neglected. That problem needs to be addressed by all of us, when and if listening is brushed over in the need to express one's thoughts without hearing the other person. Sit back and listen.

Really listen.

The Letter "M"

MEMORY

To live, to be aware of life's breath, to see sunlight skipping on the sea, to feel the sweetness of the tropical winter, to taste the bite of icy snow in winter's home, to watch a tree throb with bud before leaf's burst, these moments I cannot stop. I can only savor. Only memory stops time. But memory can slip and slide into what one wishes to recall. I search my journals for memory, for words written that day, that night, recording as witness to an event, remembering my impressions in my own handwriting. Sometimes difficult to decipher. Words seal memory.

I shout, "Stop time! Stop thief!" and wonder who steals time.

As a writer I have to remember what I have written in a linear fashion, what came first, second and third. I cannot confuse the story line, be it straight fact or my own fantasy. A writer is a storyteller. I'm reminded of Gabriel Garcia Marquez's words about his experience as a writer: "…the writing became so fluid that I sometimes felt as if I were writing for the sheer pleasure of telling a story, which may be the human condition that most resembles levitation."

Levitation indeed! For me it is the state of communion, the state of pure being, the state of bliss. It is an entry into the art of communication, into entertainment, above all the need to tell the story. And all the stories require not only imagination, but memory. Art is the ability to create and recreate from memory. After all, imagination is memory stirred, some lilting of laughter or some prick on a hideous wound. It runs the gamut from joy to tragedy. It is memory that imbues the artist to write it down, to tell it and tell it again, to repeat the favorite stories handed down from generation to generation. Story telling on the page is the writer's gift. Oral story telling is the speaker's gift, be it tribal telling or the professor at the podium, or the camp counselor telling a ghost story around a campfire to open-mouthed nine year olds. If the story is told or written with force, the reader or the listener is embroiled in the delight, the sadness, the fear, the confusion of the story. He remembers and his memory is now attached. My mother repeated and repeated family stories until they become my stories, stories to repeat to my children until they'd say, annoyed, "Mom, we know that story."

It didn't matter. The story was told once again. And memory was evoked.

When we speak of our dead, we say, '*May her memory be for blessing*'. We commemorate the date of the passing of our loved ones by lighting a *yahrzeit* candle. Wax designed to burn for 24 hours is encased in a glass and every year in memory of my mother, I light that candle. Instead of the customary *Kaddish* prayer, I sign Psalm 23 so that my mother can read my hands.

Her *yahrzeit* candle always burns far beyond the allotted 24 hours. If I awaken, half asleep in the night and see a light in the kitchen, where I keep the candle on a glass plate, I rise and go to shut off the electric light, forgetting for the moment that it is my mother's candle burning. When I see her flame, I sense her presence, slip back under the covers and sleep until the first light of morning knowing somehow she is with me. On her birthday, each year, I write her a letter. Letters that remain in my journals.

At first they were letters of sadness, then letters of longing, and later letters of family doings. Four years after her death, I wrote these words:

> *"I keep dreaming of you. I see your light. I want to write a letter in clear language, language illumined by hands, language to tell you of the birth of your great grandson, named for my father Ben, your Ben; the baby is Benjamin. He is Carrie's son, my grandson, and the great grandson of Mary and Benjamin. Benjamin Nes our newest boy bears the breath of life, bears God's breath in his nostrils. Ben boy, child of joy. Miracle child. You would love the soft folds in his young neck, but you would have never heard him cry. Are you dissolved into some unknown knowing, a knowing so deep, so infinite, that the finite portion of my life cannot understand, cannot plumb or rise to that great unknowable knowing?"*

We remember the rites of passage, moments that mark time lived. Eight days after Benjamin Nes was born, we celebrated the covenant between God and Ben, as commanded. That October day in 1993, I rose with the blessings of life, of creation and re-creation, with the blessings of a grandmother and a blessing for my grandson in my thoughts. I looked forward to greeting the invited guests who were coming to participate in the centuries old rite, the rite of the covenant. I wrote a simple blessing in my journal, *God bless you my grandson, the boy who carries my father Benny's spark, and the promise of the next generation and the generations to come.*

I remember my mother and I whisper a signed prayer for her, and I pray for the safety of my children and their children. I know that as the body ages, the parts wear away, and the need is not only to stay alive, but to keep the next generation alive, to keep the human spirit in passion, aflame.

When I look back, there is only memory. My father gone these many years, my mother five years less and I can still hear the sound of my father's deaf voice. I can hear my mother's voice, remember how she taught me the only nursery rhyme she knew, she'd sing the rhyme attempting something akin to a soprano in what she imagined was music. She was wonderful. The poem is *Baa, Baa, Black Sheep.* I see her smile, smell the sweetness of her flesh, and capture her soul in my soul. Her flesh is no more; exhumed there will be bones, skeletal remains. But within me is the sweetness of her heart, the sweetness of her demeanor, and then the memory of the rise of her temper, her temperament, the rise of indignation and anger, the sadness of life's meanness, the sadness at life's silences, the sadness of a solitary silent acceptance of a great calamity, a great infirmity—isolation in deafness and her shame, the shame of being set apart, of being misunderstood, or not understood at all.

When my daughter was in her early twenties she asked, "Mom, how did you raise us? Teach me." It was a serious question to which I never gave thought until I was summoned to give a serious answer. I learned to be a mother by example. Motherhood, I do believe, is a grace handed down from generation to generation, gifts of the past. If we are lucky as I was with a tender, caring mother, the concern continues and is built upon one mother to the next and down the line.

There are, for me, major tasks of the parent, particularly the 'Mom'. First and foremost is love. That love must be, should be, unconditional. In the first year of life, there is the physical love, the touching and the cuddling, the delicious playtime and then as the child grows older, there is the essential emotional love and support throughout his or her life.

Praise the child. Always. For his or her smile, for his face, for his work, for her joy. And the praise must be *true*. Children are not fools. Tell the child he's wonderful. He or she is indeed. No matter the age of the child, no matter the skills, no matter if they are adults with their own families; somehow, they too need and want their parents' approval. My mother thought I could do anything because I could hear, because I could negotiate in the hearing world. That confidence was both a burden and a promise that I could and would be able to function as she could not.

Play with your child. We are often so busy that we forget to play, to laugh. If my father had had oral words, if my mother could sing her song, I would hear these odes to life, *Come touch the wind. Come taste the rain. Come smell the air. Come listen to the snow fall. Come see the magic of the day. Come speak to the trees. Come tell me why you are angry. Come tell me why you cry. Come learn about everything under the sun. Come let us cook up your life's story. Come feel the wonder of you.*

I saw these beautiful commands signed, and as I put them on the page, I smile as I type their deep knowledge of the human's path to life's pleasures, their sense of play in the ordinary day, their sense of connection to the child, me, and to the world around me.

Respect the child. Children are God's gift to you, the parent, on loan. Treat them with respect and dignity and they will treat others with the same respect. They will leave one day. The wrench will be hard. But they will hopefully return bearing gifts of love, and maybe a grandchild or two to warm life's final passage. These are the moments etched in memory for children. These are the moments they will repeat to their children. They are part of family lore. My memories of my parents have sustained me through many crises.

Spend time with your children. Lots of it. Not only the oft-repeated quality time, but quantity time. Time spent with the young creates safety and security for them. A mother's presence in the next room, on the sofa nearby, bustling in the kitchen is, at times, all that is needed.

My mother said, "Time is not bankable. It is used up all at once, so spend it wisely." Those were not her exact words, the signed words do not translate well to the page. I take license and create a sentence that she might have said if she had ever heard a complete sentence.

How often have today's mothers heard the plaintive cry, "Mommy, what time will you be home?" when the baby sitter arrives and parents try to leave unobtrusively. When I was a child, there were no baby sitters. The rich had nannies and the supposed middle and working classes had relatives, particularly grandmothers. Who better to stay with a child than an adoring grandmother? Perhaps it would be best for everyone if the generations of families lived in the same city, the same town or within close traveling distance.

We are, as Americans, dispersed. Time spent with the older generation becomes more valuable, where family lore and truth is handed down and the young are rooted in the past, connected to their individual family culture. It strikes the cord of identity, a rope on which to cling, a knowing of who we are and who the child is. A little girl or a little boy might not beg to know exactly when a parent will return, not anxiously watch the hands on a clock, waiting for the moment of return and safety, when he is with his 'grandma'. Grandmothers have much to teach. Grandmothers peak positively. It is wiser to tell a child, "As soon as you clean up your room, we're going out to the park. Not,"if you don't clean your room, we're not going to the playground." I believe the difference is obvious; the first is loving and kind, the other miserable and punitive. Be honest with children. Children are not stupid. They can spot a lie and when they are quite young, it confuses them.

Educate.

Above all educate the child from the first possible moment, by touch, by taste, by closeness. Read to them. Listen to music together. Take the time to be present in their lives. Teach your children about the world in which they live. Show them a blade of grass. Stop to know the wonders of the day. Teach by example, by how you live and speak to others. Trust your child to learn. A child develops a positive self-image when he trusts the primary people in his life, most often his or her mother. And it starts early, in infancy. Before the baby realizes he is a separate entity with a separate body, he is aware that a cry of hunger or pain will bring a response. If that response is warm and attentive, the child learns to trust. It is an educational – and spiritual - milestone.

Mistakes: I've made many. We all make mistakes. It is okay, as long as we do not harm the child. And we must *apologize*. No one is perfect, not parents, not children. So relax, the rug will get dirty, the clean kitchen floor will be tracked with muddy boots, the furniture will have a new scratch and someone will lose her temper. I see my mother rapidly sign the words, "Never mind. It will be all right." And it will.

When I moved back to New York after my California

divorce, I had to work. My mother volunteered to care for my children. For two and a half years, she walked to my apartment so that I could leave early for my Brooklyn teaching position. She never missed a day. She walked in the rain, in the snow, in the sleet, in the heat. She made the children's breakfast, made them lunch at home and if I could not be home at the time of my son and daughter's dismissal time, she picked them up from school. In between, she managed her own household and was sure to take care of my father and his dinner. He loved her cooking.

Grandmothers indeed!

Perhaps she was the perfect mother. She was for me. She had uncommon common sense.

Memories come in scraps, and one memory leads to another, if we are given to ruminating about events past. What do our memories mean? Again, I don't know. But I do know that the chain of memories and the thoughts they evoke are usually part of life's lessons. In so many ways, my father was the touchstone of my young life, but as time passes, I remember my mother with an unexpected fierceness. She was part of the silent cadre of women who taught their young by example. I was her student and I remember her with a grin of pleasure. Simply, I loved her. We may lose the physical body, but the memory clings to our souls, and if we are graced, the memories arise with deep pleasure.

Mourning is done and memory takes hold. It is, as it should be.

The Letter "N"

NOURISHMENT

My mother never knew the word 'nourishment', but she knew how to nourish her family. My mother's table was a simple one. She purchased food during the years of the Great Depression on a daily basis. My father doled out the daily food allowance with care, a dollar or two. Some days there was an extra twenty-five cents; other days there was the quiet command to tell the grocer to 'mark it down in the book'. Food on credit, food from one payday to the next. Some days it was watered down soup. It fell to me to cajole the butcher to give me soup bones; they were free. Out of water, a marrow bone with bits of beef clinging to the surface, an onion, a carrot, a celery stalk, crushed tomatoes from the vegetable vendor on the corner, a solid head of cabbage from the same vendor, brown sugar and the heel of a lemon, my mother made a mighty cabbage soup, which I make to this day on cold wintry afternoons. I can smell my mother's kitchen bubbling with the warmth of the soup on the gas stove. I loved the slice of warm seeded rye bread (my job to shop at the end of the day and get two cents off the 19 cent loaf, the last one on the shelf) that I dipped into the soup. That was our Thursday night supper.

In the fall when the harvest was full, she'd mix apples, always Macintosh, she said, with purple skinned, yellow-fleshed plums. My mother peeled each apple in one continuous swirl, a bright red stream of color cascading from her paring knife. She cooked the apples and plums and a bit of lemon peel, (she loved the tartness) slowly for an hour, until we had warm applesauce for dessert. And there it was, the sweet and sour aroma of the soup and the sugary smell of the applesauce enveloped the hallway as I walked up the five stories to our Bronx apartment.

There were no formal cooking lessons. Cooking "class" consisted of one phrase when I asked, "How?" and before I could finish my sentence, she'd sign, "Watch me." I watched and in the process, her skills became mine and I became a 'foodie', fascinated with food, with the earth from which it springs, with water that feeds the soil, fascinated with nourishment, and the essential need for daily, delicious, enticing, wonderful food. Healthy food. Food necessary to nourish the body, to nourish my friends and family. So I cooked. Never a chef, but certainly a cook.

I watched her make blintzes, an eastern European crepe that she filled with sugared farmer's cheese, a white cheese akin to cottage. Her hand had many uses, one signing for language, and another was gifted with a great delicacy for cooking. She never measured anything; everything was done with her eyes. When I'd ask, "How much salt, or how much pepper?" she'd look at me with mock disdain and pour some coarse salt into the palm of her hand and create a small hill, perhaps a teaspoon in today's exact measurement, and say, "That's how much!" She'd mix water and eggs, pour flour directly from the package into the liquid for the batter. "How much flour?" I'd ask. Her answer was clear, "Until it feels right. Here is a spoon, feel it yourself."

The lessons continued. These were not lessons learned through lectures or reading. They were lessons of the eye, lessons of the senses. After I was married and we moved around from country to country, I carried my cooking lessons wherever we settled.

Each country we lived in offered me a glimpse into palettes apart from the Eastern European Jewish food I was accustomed to: Austria, Germany, Switzerland, and Spain. Above all, Spain introduced me to cooking which I then considered exotic, but is now part of the norm in my kitchen.

In Austria, I learned to perfect roasted venison larded by pure white fat to give it moisture and flavor, smothered in sour cream and onions and accompanied always by roasted potatoes, carrots and the inevitable sweet and sour red cabbage. My mother would have been horrified. "A deer, you ate a deer! Don't tell me."

In Germany, I learned to enjoy sauerbraten, sauerkraut, bratwurst and beer. At first, I turned my nose up at the heavy food, but I learned to cook the food of the land and to eat it with pleasure. My first taste of beer was thrust upon me only hours after I gave birth to my daughter. The nuns, their white wimples flying, at Munich's *Frauen Klinik* (Women's Hospital) carried in my lunch on two trays. There was much to eat: rabbit stew, a huge salted pretzel and beer, *'nahrungs bier'* nourishing beer for nursing mothers. I almost retched. A nun remained in the room with me to make sure I ate enough food. The beer was bitter, but in time, I looked forward to the meals. They kept me there for twelve days, tried to keep me in bed. I was a healthy 26-year-old woman and I did try to sneak out of bed and out of the hospital.

I did not have a delicate stomach, but our dog, a handsome brindle Boxer, could only eat cooked food. I had my first visit to another kind of butcher, one that specialized in horse meat. I incorrectly assumed that this was food for animals only. Wrong. German citizens did buy horse meat for their table. The meat was a deep burgundy color, the smell overwhelmingly sweet. Once a week, I'd buy the meat, have it ground, go home and cook it in a large pot, and as the aroma wafted through the apartment, Alex, our Boxer, would salivate and wait for me to dish it out to him. I never attempted a taste.

The food of Catalunya captivated me; it was the daily marketing in the huge open air market in Sarría where I learned to speak Spanish, to name all the shimmering, glimmering glassy eyed Mediterranean fish nestled in the outer leaves of green cabbages, to know that a purple eggplant was called a *berengena* (took me weeks to learn to pronounce that word) with some semblance of a Spanish accent. More Catalan than Castilian in

The Letter "N" NOURISHMENT

Barcelona. From the market place to the stove is a giant step that I could not have navigated without Juanita.

Juanita came to us from the field; she was a peasant in need of work. We were the recipients of her cooking skills, of her warmth and continual smiles. She was there to help with Mark when he was born. She was part of our family; she was part of that cadre of young women who were professional servants. That was then. They no longer exist. When we returned Stateside, to New York City, we left Juanita in Spain, much to my sorrow, but with excellent references.

She pounded hazel nuts with a wooden pestle into a heavy ceramic bowl which served as the base for her delicious bouillabaisse. Flour, as a thickener? She scoffed. Nuts as a thickener for the squid, mussels, shrimp and tiny *almejas* (clams), and *besugo*, a white fish similar to red snapper, was her signature dish, the dish that signaled she was an accomplished cook. Juanita insisted on flowers for the table. She set the table with rough, capable hands. And she sang. She sang the morning away, sang into her soup pot, sang until she set the house aflame with her joy.

I do not know what happened to her or where she moved after the children and I left Spain for the United States, but she is etched into every Catalan dish I prepare. I've cooked roasted whole fish stuffed with saffron rice and slivered green olives to a panache of egg tortillas (no flour): potato and onion, spinach, and tomato, three tortillas separately cooked, piled one on the other covered in a light béchamel sauce, baked for ten minutes, and served with a crisp lettuce and cucumber salad. And bread, a crusty Spanish baguette.

Then there was Claude L., an Egyptian Jew who left Cairo and his family's lucrative department store business to escape rising anti-Semitism. We met, most probably, in some café sipping strong coffee. His English was excellent, his girth rather large for a man in his early thirties, a testament to his cooking prowess. One dish of his I continue to make. It delights me and my guests with its cold-warm appeal. First, he roasted thin egg noodles in the oven on a cookie sheet, and when they were lightly toasted, golden, he slipped them into boiling lightly salted water, and cooked them until they were tender, drained them, and slid them into a large salad bowl. In advance, he prepared a salad of coarsely chopped tomatoes, cucumbers, olives, a sprinkling of parsley, a small bit of finely chopped onion, or garlic, salt and pepper, wonderful olive oil, and some wine vinegar. He poured the salad into the warm noodles, grated a half pound or more of succulent Swiss cheese, sprinkled it over the top, tossed the whole thing…and there was our evening meal. Macaroni and cheese had very close competition. A glass of wine, and some grapes, and there we were, foreign expatriates enjoying an evening, chatting up our dreams or the day's events. Food was the balm that brought us a sense of home, albeit with an unusual combination of ingredients.

When I was pregnant with my son I had a craving, a strong urge for smoked Scottish salmon. Juanita led me straight up the Calle Balmes, a rather elegant street lined with luxury apartment buildings and specialty shops scattered through the neighbor-hood. We entered a small expensive gourmet food shop. There on the counter was a side of smoked salmon, at a thousand pesetas a kilo. If it sounds like a huge amount of money, it was. I could not quite afford the roughly ten dollars a pound for the salmon when I was living on fifty dollars a month, courtesy of my ex-father-in-law. That fifty dollars had to feed me, my four-year-old daughter and Juanita, until my husband Saul returned with money in hand from his current stateside business, second hand cars. He did not return until the Christmas season, five weeks after our son was born.

In the early spring when I was barely pregnant, my parents made the trip alone from New York, to London, changed planes and found their way to Barcelona. We met them at the airport, and I marveled at my father's smarts, deaf as he was, he could maneuver around airports and manage to find his way to Europe with my mother close at his side. They loved Spain. I was their tour guide and I took them wherever they could *see* something new, something extraordinary. My father loved the bullfights, and my mother was appalled at the slaughter.

At the Plaza Catalunya, the large square at the head of the *Ramblas,* the street where the Catalans took their Sunday *paseo* (a deliberate family walk to see and be seen) Benny and Mary, my parents, were thrilled at the pace and beauty of the people, the passersby who left my parents, so often, with a smile, as they gently stared at our flashing hands. My father bought pellets of food from the Spanish Civil War veterans, either jobless, or too old to work from day to day, and fed the hundreds of pigeons, tamed by the crowds. Birds lit on his hands, and pecked directly from him. My mother, ever the cook, said, "Birds must eat too. What are they eating? Disgusting brown things."

Juanita was at the apartment on Calle Madrazo preparing our late Sunday lunch. She asked me what she should prepare. I trusted her judgment and said, "Whatever is fresh in the market, you can make for all of us." When I saw the delicate white flesh dipped in an egg batter, I didn't believe what she chose to fry. I said nothing except, "Make sure there is plenty of sliced lemon to cut any oily taste."

I did not tell either my mother or my father that the appetizer, small crisply fried whitish flesh in deep olive oil that they both relished, were in fact mountain oysters, a euphemism for a sheep's body part, testicles. We had wine to drink, bread to break, salad to crunch and sweet chocolate to end our dinner. We went to bed. In the morning, I could not contain myself, and told my mother that it was not a Mediterranean white fish that we ate. It was… Although I didn't see my father behind me, he saw my hands, turned me around to face him and signed very quickly,

"You made me eat goat's balls?"

"No Benny, they were from a sheep."

My mother, ever the peace maker, signed, "Ben, it was delicious food."

My father's mustache lifted to his prominent nose, and he

signed, "Yes, delicious." His fury tempered by the humor of the situation.

Nourishment was synonymous with love. We were gifted as children, my brother Freddie and I, with love from both our parents. For them we were magical, we could hear, we could speak. And so we could do anything, yes, anything. They nourished my brother and me with an unending love, a love that sustained us through a childhood with little material advantages, but with a solid grounding in love. That was nourishment of the soul. Food was a close second.

The Letter "O"

OPTIMISM

My mother handed me a slip of paper with the word 'optimism' printed in pencil and in capital letters. She was adamant, " Explain this word to me."

I had just arrived home from my last college class of the day, tired and hungry and had no wish to begin teaching my mother the meaning of yet another word she found enticing in her daily newspaper.

Living life is a daily act of optimism. How was I to convey that thought with my hands?

The meaning was not in my hands but in her hands. She reminded me to practice happiness every day. On most mornings as I left for my classes she Signed, "Keep happiness with you." How optimistic was that?

When my daughter Carrie was diagnosed with cancer after what appeared to be a 25-year remission from lymphoma, she apologized for having cancer a second time. I said, "We beat this before, and we can do it again."

This time I was not certain, I did not have the optimism I had in the years past. Would an optimistic outlook coupled with love heal Carrie of this second bout of disease? Carrie lived on optimism, and at times, I was imbued with her sense of living on and on to old age. I almost believed she would survive this second onslaught.

She carried us along with her beliefs, with her prayers, and we were willing participants in her outrageous, courageous optimism. Both my parents were gone. Would they have joined Carrie in her optimism? I shall never know. That optimism had been a major force in keeping her alive. I continued the legacy handed to me by Benny and Mary: nourish with love, nourish with food for Carrie and her teen-age children, Ben and Sarah. They too, were carried along with her optimism, with her hope. Her children believed her pronouncements, her certainty that her life would continue, and she would be their mother for a very long time, at least until she could share in the life of another generation.

For all the years I lived on the East Coast, Carrie and I were separated by a continent. She lived in Los Angeles with her young family then added the greater part of an ocean when she moved to Honolulu. We spoke almost every day, about the mundane and the significant, about husbands and holidays, about children and their cats, above all about our connection, mother and daughter, friend and friend, confidante to confidante. We were there for each other. We shared life, in all its perils, all its joys, and all our talks for the future. We were optimistic. That was then.

There were pitfalls, some small, some large: divorce for

Carrie, for yet a third time, homework left undone by Ben or Sarah, braces and dentists, finding furniture for the Hawaiian house. It was a beautiful house, different from anything on the mainland. It faced the volcanic mountains, lush with green life, devoid of animal predators, and on many mornings, soft clouds cascaded down the hillside burning off with the late morning sun exposing the clear blue of an island in the Pacific. The plumeria tree at the front steps of the house was a marvel of yellow blooms and sweet scent that invaded the house.

It was Hawaii. Beautiful. Carrie wanted furniture that was roomy and comfortable, furniture that one could nestle in, furniture that said, "Come on in, and have a seat. Listen to the sounds of the baby grand piano as my family plays in the center of the house." Ben had magic in his fingers. He would touch the keyboard and play until we stopped, until we all sat and listened, while Sarah, still very young, her head bent over her canvas, drew her amazing illustrations; all fantasy. Their talents were visible at the outset; their abilities to express themselves. Yet in all this burgeoning, gifted family, Carrie's third marriage, which held such promise, withered with a partner unwilling to fully enter the bond.

In the spring of the year before she and her husband parted, I visited, hoping the marriage could be resurrected. By then, he had moved out, although he came to visit, perhaps to pretend that there was something still viable. Relief at his departure was palpable. The children were pleased that he was gone, and they were a family of three again, and I, Nana, was very welcome. Carrie insisted on living her life publicly as though nothing was untoward, insisting that we go forward to the health food stores, to Whole Foods, and feed ourselves. She delighted in pointing out the Hawaiian delicacies, to pointing out fruits native to island palates. There was bounty in food and people. There were attachments to others. People adored Carrie, or ignored her, missing her light. She offered bounty and would not accept illness as part of her life's biography.

When she told me of her bouts with 'food poisoning,' I sensed that her diagnosis was not accurate. Carrie was effusive and warm in her contact with the emergency room physicians that cared for her when she arrived by ambulance, charming them with her wit and uncanny intelligence. This time to her detriment.

Life was forever. She was attached to the living and would live to take care of me in my old age as I took care of her when she had had lymphoma in her early thirties. I knew how to take care of her, but now she had two young children. I put my intuition aside, and allowed Carrie to play the lead role in this, her denial of a probable serious disease.

Her public face and her private face seemed to mesh, but when I found her, with her head in the toilet, retching, I openly challenged her to seek expert medical help.

"Oh Mom, it's something I ate. Remember that roadside stand at the beach, I probably picked up something there."

I asked, "How many times have you had food poisoning,

and from how many restaurants in the past year? And what of Ben and Sarah, did they get sick?"

She ignored me.

Was it optimism or foolishness?

"Mom, you're leaving in a few days and we have to have fun. I know how you love the beach. We could go near sundown, let the kids swim and get something at the bar, a sandwich, or some fried fish. The food is good and we can relax and you can enjoy Hawaii."

I shook my head. "Not a good idea, not this afternoon."

"I'll prepare a dinner picnic. I'm fine."

I relented.

We piled into Carrie's old white van and she drove around the Island until we reached Waimanolo Beach, a favorite of Ben and Sarah's. The water was clear and the sand underfoot was like manna to my urban feet. I dug my toes into the silky sand. If one could describe happiness, it was a late afternoon at this exquisite four-mile stretch of sand and water. Parking the van was easy.

Hanauma Bay was another favored beach, and Carrie insisted we go. Hanauma Bay is a nature preserve, filled with wondrous sea creatures, especially the large green sea turtles. The Bay is ringed by a tuff, almost a complete circle outlining the blue water. Tourists are crowded together in the low-lying sun-light. I had wanted to go, but I didn't want to disturb Carrie's quiet time. Each time I relented with misgivings. I thought, *she should be resting, recovering from that bout with her so-called food poisoning.* I became accustomed to her psychic strength, her will, her unending optimism. It had carried her through much adversity. It would sustain us in the future.

There were life lessons in her behavior, but I did not recognize them, not then. There was opportunity to be seized, an earlier diagnosis, perhaps better medical care. When I left for the mainland and my solitary existence in Florida, I put my worries aside, but they began to enter my consciousness. Carrie and I continued our lengthy phone conversations, especially when both her children were busy. The six-hour time difference did interfere, but we managed to keep the tie that bound us robust.

Yet, I knew from the timbre of her voice, and sometimes when her voice trailed off at the end of a sentence and I could not distinguish her vowels from consonants, that she was ill. When I questioned her about her health, she said that she was fine, annoyance in her tone. Once again I backed off. I should not have. As optimistic as she was, I was not. My inner being shouted it was otherwise. But, still, I remained silent. Optimism has its rewards. Reality is truth. *Carpe diem. Seize the day*, seize the opportunity that presents itself. That too is optimism.

When Carrie left the Island, left her beautiful house behind, and sold most of her furniture and bulky possessions and headed for my home in Western Massachusetts to begin treatment, to rest and recover, she was full of plans for her future and for the education of her children. Her stay with me would be at most a year, until she got her bearings and her health straightened out, and she would begin again. The promise of life beckoned. I encouraged her courage. I promised myself that it would be the last time I would be a caretaker, the last time I would put my life on the back burner. I had other books to write, other students to teach. We'd be on our way, Carrie to do the television show she always talked about, and me to continue writing and having fun, a bit fearful as the ravages of aging were looming in the not too distant future. She'd find a house or an apartment equidistant between New York and Boston, or she would move once again to Los Angeles where she had lived for 25 years.

Oh there were plans afoot. I would come along and live with my family, and she'd find a rich older gentleman, a left over from the film industry, to fill out my days with companionship. Yes, I would live in my own house or apartment. We laughed at the thought of Mom tagging along.

I had my doubts.

Her optimism, in the end, did not carry her through a long life.

Optimism is necessary for all of us. Optimism is the optimal coping mechanism. When all else seems impossible, hope and a forward looking attitude can usually carry us through to the next beginning. My optimism, learned from Carrie, now resides in her children. They will find their way, both Ben and Sarah. Hopefully their dreams will carry them through. If they persist, if they have absorbed their mother's courage and determination, they will find their own paths.

The Letter "P"

PURPOSE

In the first month of the year 1981, I watched a television interview with the playwright Lillian Hellman. When she was asked about what she expected from the rest of her life, her answer was swift: "I want to live as long as possible, as comfortably as possible, with as much work as possible." I found this quote in one of my handwritten journals stuck into the margin alone without any qualifying remarks.

Today, as I write this, I am struck by the word 'purpose'. Was Lillian Hellman speaking to the purpose of her life? The question that one often hears and ponders on is: What is the purpose of my life? I've heard many answers, none quite so telling as Lillian Hellman's.

To be an artist is a gift given to few and the gift carries with it a responsibility to explore and express that gift in whatever form it may take. I am compelled, with pleasure, to put pen to paper. These days, however, I have taught myself to write directly on the computer, although my notes are always written by hand. There is that specific quality that I believe moves from my brain, down my arm to my left hand to my pen. Out flows the ink onto the page, my thought or thoughts given some permanence. I think too of the painter, the draftsman, the violinist, the pianist, all dependent upon their arms and hands to create the work that they have been given to do.

Hands do work. Persistence and patience are the hallmarks of work. To list the work done by human hands would fill up pages: A few examples include the farmer and the housewife, the chauffeur and the pilot, the teacher and the student, the lover and the loved, the mother and the child and the list goes on. Each of us can compile our own lists.

I rise from my bed each morning with a sense of optimism, knowing there is work for me, work that may be tedious, but it is my work, my way of living my day. I think back to the places where I lived. My first memory of place is Brooklyn where we lived until I was 6 and then moved to the Bronx. I understood that there was work for me to do, but without any awareness of the role I was to play when we left and moved to an apartment on Simpson Street.

I'd become a full-fledged 'parentified child' without naming my work. All the 'hearing' family members, my grandmother and my aunts - my support system - were at least an hour away by subway. Morning into morning, day into day, and night into night passed, and the years passed and I signed and interpreted and protected my parents as I grew into my teen years and on into college. Later when I sat down to write about that time, these words about my father fell from my left hand onto the page, ink smudged, as notes for a memoir or novel:

BRONX SILENCE

"So many stories have been squeezed out of Bronx buildings. I was born to tell one more tale. Not something out of the ordinary, not something extraordinary. Yet, something different. I was born into deafness. Not the deafness of the old who cup their hands over their ears and say, 'Whaddya say?" No, not that.

It was of another kind, the kind of silence that wraps around the body, the silence that seeks hidden corners, the silence that never leaves. The silence that stuffed me into an envelope and licked it shut. The silence that never heard a shout, at least, not mine. And now that I am older, I crave the silence. Silence is safe. There are no intruders, no one to disturb the quiet mind.

Quiet. Long and slow. Quiet that enshrouds me. Quiet that I long to hold. Who can hold quiet? 'Tis not a corporeal thing. The Bronx building, five stories high, held together with brick and mortar…that's a thing. That has substance, embodies. Filled with bodies. They are unquiet. They move around their rented rooms. They cook and eat, fornicate and deliver.

They cannot deliver sound. The sound of music. The sounds of life. I was born into deafness, but I am not deaf. I lived among the deaf as one lives among ghosts denied speech. Oral speech. And when hands are tied, the Deaf are mute. But I have a mouth and I have ears that hear and I have, yet, a tale to tell.

A single stroke, a menningal stroke snaked down his spine and silence was his name. Blind and deaf he was. 'Twas not a game. No, not at all. But I cannot shut my ears to sound. I try. Sound seeps in, unbidden, birdsong and child-song, fire-song and tire-song. Name the uninvited sounds. Too many, too many. Sounds outside the boy's ken.

Unheard, rarely understood. Longing seized his soul, the soul of young Ben. He reached for a word, but there was no word for music to strike the heart of the child who could not hear, who never heard a single musical note.

And when he was a man, he strained to hear. He teased God, cupping his right hand to his ear as the old ones do, daring Him to open the gates of sound. God does not answer foolish pleas. No, not God. He granted one miracle. The young Ben had his sight restored. He kept his sight until his death. And with his eyes he heard what other men could not.

Bronx silence was his playground. In this vast paved city, Ben the man chided God and man with laughter. So we laughed and called him Benny. I was born to Benny and his beautiful wife, Miriam, born into the land of silence. Silence so vast, it was without end.

Within that silence, magic reigned. Benny's silent raucous voice, a voice that attempted speech, pealed with pleasure. With my feet on his, we danced, Benny and I, to the sound of his music, to the tempo of his life.

Joy was his, and he, in silence, gifted me."

Both my father Benny and I had work. His was to raise me with joy, to raise me without fear of the unnamed sound. He took me on his days off by bus and by train to all the city streets that he loved. He taught me to love the place in which I lived. I hold that awe for most of the places I have lived, on the North American continent and on the European.

The places I have lived, each city, each street and each house has left an indelible imprint on my being. The first foreign place I lived in was Vienna, not too long after World War II. It began in the early autumn of 1954. Today Vienna is a healed city; then it was reeling from the shock and deprivation of war's aftermath. The city smelled. The people smelled. Soap was, for some, still a luxury. If I attempted a smile at a passerby, I was ignored. Soon, like the rest of the populace, I walked with my head down, bucking the wind. I walked the streets in the cold winter, my heavy great coat keeping me from freezing. I wrote my mother, in the simplest declarative sentences, and told her how cold we were, how the small coal fire between our bedroom and the living room did not last the night.

Within two weeks, a package came from my mother. She sewed two red flannel night-shirts, one for me and one for my husband. Saul and I were poor but filled with hope for the days to come. Perhaps he would find work as a foreign correspondent at the London or Paris bureau. Maybe Moscow. But the only work he could find before the harsh winter set in was as a stringer for International News Service (INS now UPI, United Press International), for the grand sum of 17 American dollars a week in the Vienna bureau. The bureau chief, we were sure, was an ex-German officer in the Wehrmacht.

I had to find work, we had to eat more than hairy stored carrots, old cabbage and wrinkled potatoes. We had to stay warm. We had to buy sacks of coal for the grate that connected our two rooms on the Strozzigasse and I, with feigned confidence as a trained teacher, went directly to the University of Vienna. The administrator put me in touch with the Austro-American Institute and I was hired at once to teach English to professionals, dentists and lawyers, businessmen and women, hoping to immigrate to Canada, Australia and the United States. So began yet another career. I was 23 years old.

Teaching became incidental to our lives as couriers of goods smuggled across the German border to Spain and Italy. The cover was good. Saul's American passport read: *journalist.* Mine read: *teacher.* This was not ordinary smuggling. These were not ordinary people.

Everyone we worked with was a Jewish survivor of the war. They were peripheral Holocaust victims and they were young. All of them were still in their twenties. Some lived as Christians with false papers, others in the sewers of Warsaw, and still others in the forests foraging for food and for their lives. I didn't ask the 'how' question, How did you survive for so many years without sustained sustenance? I listened and waited for scraps of information over a cup of Viennese coffee, over a slice of bread and cheese at an evening meal. Bit by bit, I learned what they had to teach me.

The first teaching was offered by a private student who wanted to polish his English hoping one day, like my other students, to reach the United States. He was referred to me by the Austro-American Institute. Our first meeting was tentative. I was uncertain, timid about arriving alone in his landlady's apartment reeking of old furniture and cooked onions. He was polite, correct in every way. He questioned my credentials. I was barely out of college with two years of teaching experience in the slums of Harlem. But I liked him.

He said at last, "You may call me by my first name, Samuel."

"And I am Ruth."

"You have a name from the Bible."

"Yes, I am Ruchal." This is my Yiddish name.

"So, you are Jewish."

The connection was immediate. We met once, sometimes twice a week. His English was good, and when I asked him where he learned to speak so well, he said, "In the schools of course, but as a Jew my education was ended by the Nazis when I was 13. There was no future for Jews in Cracow. Why not kill them all? We hid in the forest and ate what we could when we could. When the war was over we left the forests without any professions, we had no training, no skills. We needed to eat and we learned quickly about the black market. I worked with the American GIs. A soldier gave us a cigarette to sell and English words to speak. One cigarette became two and soon we had money and every day, one or two more words to speak. There is my English."

He was meticulous. His clothes were of the best Italian man-ufacture, probably hand sewn. His finger nails were newly man-icured each time we met. His cologne was subtle, but thankfully masked his landlady's roasting pork and sauerkraut. I wanted to know about his transformation from a four-year forest survivor to this stylish man. I dared not ask.

Months passed and Samuel's wife Erna (not her true name) came to visit. She was shy of me, the rich American girl. How was I to tell her that I would walk by Demel's Viennese bakery and press my nose to the glass because I couldn't afford one of their famous pastries? Erna would leave then and return to Munich to see her doctors. No reason was given. Nothing spe-cific occurred, nothing was said, yet there was a sense of trust between me and Samuel.

By then I knew part of his story. Samuel was, I believe now, the leader of a small group of men that smuggled loose silver and gold bullion to Milan and Barcelona where these goods were difficult if not impossible to obtain legally.

Finally Samuel asked to meet my husband, "An American journalist? He's Jewish?"

"Yes," I reassured him.

We met that evening at a local café. Samuel was looking for clean couriers to drive across the borders. Saul and I were ready to be part of this clandestine group of men who salvaged and used their survival skills to earn a living and provide funds for returning stateless Jews. These people were in need of hospital care and general assistance. We were a perfect team. We had no

European background, no connection to anyone. All we needed was a professional car. Samuel would provide that, provided we moved to Munich, Germany where he was able to legally buy gold and silver from German banks.

For me, this was to be important work, a way to help. But first the move to Munich and a job on a news desk in Radio Free Europe for Saul. To this day I do not know how Samuel arranged the new position. I can only assume that he did. And on a cold February day in 1955 we moved to an apartment in the building apparently owned or leased by Radio Free Europe.

Munich was a city relentlessly on the move. Vienna lumbered. Austria was an occupied country and every month I watched as the occupying powers strutted their military strength handing the rein of control over to one of the four military commands: the Russians to the Americans, the Americans to the British, the British to the French, and so it was until Austria was declared sovereign once again. But Munich, still occupied by the four Allied powers was a city clamoring for rebirth, rebuilding bombed out structures. Piles of bricks still littered some streets. People streamed from one end of the downtown area to the other, always in orderly fashion.

I found it psychologically difficult to speak the language of Adolph Hitler, but in time, I did learn to speak rudimentary German, "küche Deutch" (kitchen German). I made errors, without doubt, but I kept on speaking, kept on communicating. I learned then that one thinks differently in another language. I attempted to read the newspaper. I understood about

50% of what I read. The paper kept me in contact with the local news. There was no television. Radio voices were too fast for me to understand completely. But it was all language and it kept me tethered to the street on which I lived, the *Academiestrasse.* The building housed the employees of Radio Free Europe, a building filled with expatriates from all parts of Europe, particularly refugees from the Communist regimes of East Germany and the Soviet Union.

Academy Street was home to the Munich Art School. The street was wide, the school beautiful. Yet there was still organized piles of rubble in the streets, remnants of a war that had ended in 1945. Students ranged from older teen-agers to young adults. Even they were not approachable, they traveled in cliques, or there were the solitary ones who kept to themselves. Each frigid morning many of them gathered in the *molkerei,* the milk shop, where they had their tin cans filled with warm milk from huge metal milk containers, probably fresh from the local farms. Some bought newly laid eggs, stuck a pin into the head of the egg and sucked out breakfast. I turned away from the sight of a raw egg sliding down someone's gullet. When I was in the shop, attempting to find a friend, someone with whom I could chat, I hesitated to speak my fractured German, concerned that I would be ridiculed. That had happened in several shops.

In all my attempts to connect to a German friend, I found I did not; I could not. I could speak the language at a minimal level yet somehow when I walked down a street, I could not help but wonder at the 30 and 40 year old male passers-by, comfortably talking to one another, comfortable in their city, wonder whether that single individual had a hand in murdering anyone of 60 of my relatives in Eastern Europe. That did keep me from forming any relationships. I kept to myself and to the American expatriate community that worked at Radio Free Europe. I roamed the beautiful city of Munich alone rather than trust myself with a casual slip of the tongue.

So we began our double life. On odd weekends we drove south to Italy and Milan where we unloaded our car of silver cargo from Italian crafted secret compartments of in the outer courtyard of a jewelry factory. We drove across Western Europe to Spain where gold bullion was the currency of demand, then $32 an ounce. During the week, we maintained our façade as the young ambitious American couple eager to be part of the European media scene.

Italy was wonderful, but it was Spain that captured us. The drive to Spain took twenty hours and five stops for coffee, for customs inspection and for gas. There was Barcelona, a city in rhythm, a city of music, of Gaudian fairytale architecture, a city redolent of olive oil and frying fish, a city of elegant women exquisitely dressed, of men who patted each other on the back greeting one another with a strong embrace. Barcelona was the city that drew me to my own nexus. Barcelona was that city I would ache for when I was back in Germany, goods delivered, cash in hand, to give to Samuel.

It was also a city torn by the Spanish Civil War. It was the proving ground for German bombers; the first European city to be bombed. Downtown buildings bearing bullet pock marks were the only evidence of that brutal war.

Barcelona was a city in full recovery. Days shone with sunlight and the nights were cool, the gypsy cadence, the foot stomping flamenco, the sounds of lyrical Spanish, foreign, yet familiar, soothed. There was the lure of late night dinners at restaurants that served tiny white eels in tiny clay casseroles. There was succulent paella rich with chicken, sausages and fruits of the sea. There was food and there was wine, and one day Saul left me for a Spanish woman. But that was later, years later. A decade later. After our children were born.

I decided, finally, after the years abroad, to return home, to my place, to the place that first marked me, to the city in which I was born. In one of my journals I found this writing from a hotel window in New Jersey, a writing I did at the moment:

a bright pink dawn over Manhattan. The Empire State Building's spire, grey concrete-- window refracted light stands sentinel over the city that stretches across the horizon. An urban ocean of brick and mortar. And the dawn light leaves, the sun glints no more. And now the cool freshness of day, the buildings sky-blue gray, monuments, markers to the lives within. I look across to 34th Street. And soon will come the city beat, the rapid march of feet, thudding from subway and bus, from cars and trucks, for the rich, for the swift and those down on their luck; the homeless soon will shuffle

off their tattered night's coverings, collect their mental ill-
nesses, their drunkenness, their forgotten souls in hand and
reach for a handout. But for now the city lies still, unable
to rouse itself from the weekend's play. Ah, here a truck
moves, another and another, a lone car, white, and now
a black one. The Hudson lies between here and there, the
river hidden by houses and palisade, by railroad track, and
by chimney stack. I love this city where the living move and
the dead lie. And I want to know why I have left? Why?"

The alarm rang and I left my morning writings to begin the
day, but I had a clear sense of home. I was back. Back to begin
again. This time with two young children in tow, a boy and a
girl and a life to discover day by day. Unafraid. Most of the time.

Every writer needs an address, a place from which to spring,
to think. I did believe I would do some of my best writing in
my one bedroom Queens apartment overlooking a small patch
of lawn. Instead, I taught classes in a junior high school and in
a city college to pay my rent and feed my children. My writing
was cathartic, not art. I left it for a better time and place, a place
where I would have a sense of quiet, where there would be vast
stretches of green in the spring and I would be healed of a sad
divorce, able then to know the craft of writing. It was later that
I became fully acquainted with the 'sentence'.

A sentence is a narrow band of thought. Most lives are lived
in a narrow band of experience, a narrow corridor of time, of
place, of person. Some sentences fly at one. Some sentences

sneak up on one. Some sentences are best left unnoticed. And some sentences slide into an unconscious, subconscious realm, shelved and put away to be taken out and turned over in a moment of absolute quiet, in that moment alone.

Each sentence is a new beginning for me, for any writer. I do not think of structure, which if I stop to examine is diaphanous, amorphous, and slippery, in danger of the hairline crack in the clay maquette, in danger of splitting apart before it is cast in bronze, before the pages are bound between two hard covers. I do not stop; the writing flows. The page, blank and beautiful to start with, holds the complete thought, the shaping, the rounding, the molding, the painterly qualities of words, the musical notes of words, melodic in sentences, in paragraphs. Oh beautiful words. Ah, the love of the sentence. Writing is not a 'fool's paragraph'. It is the moment of grace, the moment of me, unadorned.

All sentences, especially those strung together, tell a story. And that was to be my work, to tell the story not only of my life, but also of the lives of others, both in fiction and non-fiction. It continues to be my work. Unfinished to the end.

I learned to write on the backs of envelopes, in ink, in pencil. My first writings were on the backs of neatly folded brown paper bags fresh from the corner Brooklyn grocery. My mother began my penmanship-comprehension lessons. There are no exact dates. I can only assume that I was 4 years old, perhaps a bit younger. I could read the letters of the alphabet that she signed. Now it was time to have me read the printed letters that matched the signed ABCs and then with little hands write the letters and in time read letters that formed words and later sentences. I remember those afternoons with my mother and a glass of milk and rye bread and butter that she placed before me, she said for energy, while I learned to write every letter of the alphabet. That was then. Later, I learned to write on my knee, on a restaurant table, on the back of a menu, on a snowy Canadian night by fireplace glow, in my kitchen sipping hot tea.

By the late 1960's, I was remarried and living in wintry Toronto. I continued to write most days, penning my life, my imagination and my thoughts to paper. Years later when my Florida house was girdled by a ring of intense summer heat, a boundary not to be crossed in midday when the sun struck like a snake, I wrote. I avoided the tropic's intensity. I looked out my window into the garden at the areca palm fronds fanning the yard into mock coolness and knew that I was sealed into an air conditioned space where I could work without interruption.

I had another place. I had work. Stories to tell. The apparent emptiness of working in a quiet space alone in a room was and *is* abundant with life. It will always be. I had work; I had purpose.

I persisted. Lillian Hellman persisted, my father persisted; Samuel persisted. We persisted in living our lives. They are only three of the many who have had the bravery to persist, to carry on, to understand their purpose, to live a life of their own choosing.

My children, Carrie and Mark, were yet to be born.

The Letter "Q"

QUIET

The words *y'did nefesh* refer to God as a soul companion. My mother was my soul companion. She taught me her way of God, a silent way.

When I am in need of comfort, I comfort myself by seeking *quiet*, a space for my body and soul to rest. A moment or two to commune with my soul companion without the din of responsibility. Sometimes I am aware of God's presence within me, sometimes not. Most often, within that quiet realm, I think of my mother and feel her presence. I remember the connection. In her death state, she is somehow alive, there. Aware. I do not petition for anything. I am quiet. As she is.

Quiet is essential, restorative. A life lived so busy, so crammed with detail, at times frantic with pressure to get things done, whatever they may be, interferes with the moments of self, the moments to commune not only with oneself but with one's essential life force.

Questioning the quiet, the reason for being, does not apply. It is. I am content in the quiet, content to be, grateful for the silent moments, the moments that enhance me, that allow me to rise and continue the day. Quiet is rest. Rest is required.

One fall day I asked my friend Norman Ringel as we walked and talked on a downtown Toronto street, "What is the meaning of the word *Shabbat* (Sabbath)?"

"Rest," he said.

I was stunned by his answer. So simple.

I am not literate in the depths of learning required for a rabbi, not conversant with the Talmud as much as I would like to be, but when I walk into a synagogue I am infused with quiet. Some may call it peace. For me, it is complete stillness. Awe, perhaps.

I have entered a community of quietness, a safe haven where, in the presence of my community, I am whole. I am grateful to be in the presence of grace.

I find that quiet when the first tentative light of day slips into my bedroom. I am awake, mindful of the entry of a new beginning. A new day. I am a morning person; some would call me a lark. I do listen for that first bird call. Soon I hear the cacophony of bird song and I am filled with pleasure. I am quiet. I listen for the sounds of life stirring about me, a sudden rustle of a wind catching a branch, the surprising peck-peck of the red headed woodpecker against the trunk of a mighty slash pine tree.

It is life renewed daily.

GATHER UNTO ME

gather unto me
the day unfolding, to give, to hold, to be
silent, serene
rain pelts against the window,
silent, demanding
solid, helmeting rain
gather unto me the quiet within
grand silence, marred by thunder
struck by a golden slash
gather unto me rest, repose
the tropical storm that is harmony
the deluge sings its own song
a rhythm to please the soul
gather unto me my soul
press me into the quiet of the day
afternoon dark as night
dark unto me, glory of the day
of the sluicing day
erasing yesterday
the day cleansed
gather unto me

Carrie now inhabits the world of silence, alone, up on a hill in
Western Massachusetts. After days of intense grief, I'd talk to
my mother and tell her to gather Carrie to her, to look after

her. She was, after all, new to the world of the dead. How did I dare intrude on the world of silence? My mother handed me my soul, as I had handed Carrie her soul with her birth. It was her birthright. So we are soul linked, mother to daughter, daughter to daughter, and the link continues, generation to generation. We are linked by the mystery of the soul, the quiet that contains our holy spirit.

The Letter "R"

RENEWAL

Sometimes we are graced with an opportunity that was lost along the way. My childhood friend Estelle Applebaum and I slipped apart during our early adolescence when she moved from the Bronx back to Brooklyn. She was old enough to prepare her own lunch, old enough to live with her parents once again. Her mother Hinde, who worked in a yeshiva with an apron across her round belly, was so obsessed with continual hand washing, she was unable to feed her daughter. Her father Nathan noticed that his young daughter was not thriving and so he took her to see the local doctor. Estelle was starving. By the time Estelle was three, she had to be spoon fed water by strangers who took her in for the daily dollar her father Nathan paid for her care. It was, according to Estelle, a Cinderella story. She was not treated well in that household. Hers was a stolen childhood.

I remember Nathan well. I remember him as the kind grey-faced cobbler, the shoemaker with the generous heart who, when he came to visit Estelle, I'd see his weathered face slowly gather a smile and then the wide grin of pleasure at seeing his youngest child as he walked down Dawson Street.

By the time Estelle was nine years old, she was living with her married brother Dave and his wife Sarah. Dave was an amputee and wore a prosthesis. He was run over by a milk wagon soon after his parents emigrated from Poland to the United States. Sarah had polio and her legs were encased in braces and she swung her upright body on crutches as she maneuvered through her days. They were both wonderful. Their handicap was for me, quite normal.

Estelle and I were children together. Playmates. We wore our green Girl Scout uniforms and went to meetings I do not remember. But I do remember our closeness. We each had ten cents to buy a Charlotte Russe (a round bit of sponge cake, topped with whipped cream and a cherry, all propped up in a paper cup) and a hot dog at the local delicatessen after the meeting. To this day Estelle and I speak of that evening treat. She tells me that there is a bakery nearby that makes our girlhood favorite and one day we will have to have one.

When Dave and Sarah found work during World War II with the IRS in Washington D.C., we were devastated. Would they leave and take Estelle with them? I overheard Dave and Sarah's concern about what to do with Estelle. I told my mother this news with great sadness. My mother was quick. She signed, "Your friend can live with us. You are both small and you can share your bed." I don't believe I let her finish her thoughts. I know I ran to Sarah and Dave's apartment to tell Estelle that she didn't have to move, that she could stay with us.

She was with us for almost two years. Nathan insisted on paying for Estelle's keep. My mother refused, telling me that she could always add more water to the soup, that she could afford another potato. Nathan won out. I don't remember how much was offered and it no longer matters.

When Estelle returned to Brooklyn we wrote to each other. Letters that no longer exist. Time passed and the letters stopped. I graduated from high school and college married Saul and went off to live in Europe for almost 10 years. Estelle married Jerry at 18. He was 19. I learned this later, a half a century later.

When my book IN SILENCE was published in late 1990, there were many book reviews, many articles about me, photographs. The Miami Herald ran an article that was almost a full page of the story IN SILENCE, a large photo of me and an insert of my parents' picture. Sarah Applebaum recognized my mother and father and called my husband who was at home alone in Florida. I was on a book tour, speaking and signing books at a bookshop in Moscow, Idaho and staying at my son's home in Orofino, Idaho for a few days before I headed for Los Angeles and Seattle and an opportunity to see my grandchildren.

I can recall the conversations verbatim. My husband Richard said, "Sarah Applebaum called. Do you know who she is?"

"Yes! Where is she?"

"She's in Florida. Not too far from the house."

He gave me Sarah's phone number. I called immediately. Dave had a sudden heart attack and died outside a bank while she waited for him on the other side of the street. But Estelle was living in Florida.

And there it was. The renewal of something surely lost and found. These are the words I wrote after meeting Estelle for the first time:

"Estelle and I met for lunch. The intervening fifty years etched in our faces and we spoke of our lives, we spoke as sisters, although we are not. The knots of childhood remain, impenetrable, linking us as family. We spoke over seared chicken sandwiches, tea and crumbed apple pie (without cream) that we shared. We spoke of scarred children, ourselves, spoke of strong women, ourselves, hidden, hidden as women, hidden as children.

"We spoke calmly and well, recognizing that there is no return like the return to one's youth, to one's beginnings. This friendship creates family, a sense of identity. She has no one else who remembers her as a child, except Sarah. (Sarah died several years after this excerpt from my journal was written.)

"Estelle needed to unburden. I did too. She used the phrase 'scarred child' several times. Yes, scarred and strong. Scarrings created strength for us, but silence as well. No one knew us.

"When we parted I said, "Seeing you is a gift from God." We moved toward one another and hugged.

"We're family", she said. "I have no one else left from those early years."

Today Estelle has a husband, two daughters, three grand-sons and me, an old friend.

We cannot recover the lost years. What we have is now. What my daughter Carrie had was 'now'. Recovery from the chemotherapy, the powerful poisonous drugs that destroyed her lymphoma also paralyzed one of her vocal chords. Her lyrical singing voice, her musical instrument was reduced to a whisper, a forced sound with only one vocal chord. Grateful for her life, I said little. I spoke of her loss only with her doctor. The odds were not good. Vocal chord recovery was highly unlikely. And then one day, a miracle. At least for me.

In order for her to shower, I had to wrap her arm in plastic wrap lest the catheter and the port for her drugs became wet. We argued about something that morning. I know not what. We were both tired, snappish. I wrapped her arm, warned her to keep it out of the shower and left for her small kitchen to prepare breakfast.

Standing at the stove, I heard singing. Carrie? Slowly, I walked back to the bathroom, never mind burnt scrambled eggs, singed toast. I heard her voice in song. Carrie was singing. She had her voice back. Spontaneous remission. No explana-tion. It simply was. It was not only a thrilling recovery, but a sense that she and I, both of us, could and would be able to renew our lives, live apart but be close. These thoughts did not occur to me as I wept silently, but I felt a lifting of the burden of care. She would recover. She kept singing in that shower until I said, "Enough, Carrie, don't tax that vocal chord too, too much." We laughed. As she stepped out of the shower, I unwound the plastic wrap around her arm.

Fast forward, almost two years later to Irene Humphrey's apartment. Irene Humphrey was a renowned singing coach. From my journal, these are the words, that I wrote on December 13, 1991 when we first met her:

When she opened the door to the small dark hallway, the entry way into her apartment, I saw with shock the epitome of a sweet old lady, the image conjured by society: short white hair, a fringe of sparse bangs, a two strand pearl choker at the base of her slender neck complementing her plain cream silk blouse tucked into her taupe ultra suede skirt. I raised my eyes to meet hers and was startled to hear the strength of her soprano 'spinto' speaking voice reach across to me with such pleasure. She held my large hand in her small arthritic one.

"Come in, come in."

We followed her down the short dark corridor covered in what I assume was an old Italian tapestry from floor to ceiling. In the corner stood a five-foot wrought iron candelabra.

"Is that a menorah?"

"No, it's not. Beautiful thing isn't it?"

Irene Humphrey had candelabras everywhere: silver ones and two more large ones in her living room flanking her antique Jacobean desk. Golden shag carpeting was from another decorating era. Windows were shuttered and closed, floor to ceiling and painted pewter blue. Soft.

On the wall adjoining her kitchen, where she never cooked, was her piano.

"I had a baby grand in my house," she said, "but I couldn't take it to my apartment after Stetson (her husband) died. So I sold it. I have a piano broker who told me about this one; it's from Ede, Holland. He said, "Take it, try it, live with it. You see it has its harp upright." She stroked it.

The beautiful burnished wood rose from the floor like a flat Henry Moore sculpture, sinuous, curved—holding sound, holding music within its shape.

When I told her I was tone deaf she said, "I don't believe it."

She leaned over and with her knarled index finger played one note after the other and said, "Sing it!"

I did: It was perfect.

So, I thought secretly to myself, I should find a music teacher, someone to teach me to control my breath. I am touched by women who spend their lives in music, a discipline so far removed from my writing life, and yet somehow akin.

As Irene walked back into the room carrying a tray, I thought—She's one of the old ones now. Her gait is not what it was when she made her debut as Mimi at La Scala Opera House in Milan, Italy when she was eighteen years old. My guess is that she is in her mid-seventies, but I would *never ask. She also asked me the secret of my white teeth. Hers are her own, but they have yellow-brown caste. They look tobacco stained, but I know without asking that she, a singer, never smoked. Not Irene Humphrey.*

The lesson began. Carrie lay down on the beige beach towel in the middle of the living room to begin her breathing exercises, exercises to strengthen her tone using her diaphragm instead of her throat, exercises to keep the breath behind the note, exercises to eliminate throat clearing.

Carrie ran through some warm up exercises—hey there, hey there, hallelujahs--, her voice and body moving in music. She removed her magenta angora sweater and stood in her gray tights and white tee shirt, body beautiful and voice beautiful. She sang popular tunes. When she sang an aria, Babbo Pieta, from Puccini's La Bohème with her colorful emotionally charged lyric soprano voice, I kept my tears to myself.

Irene Humphrey applauded Carrie's progress after only five lessons. "That was so much better than the last time."

It was beautiful. Irene said with a phrase here, a word there—'put your breath behind it'—'lightly'—'have fun with this elevated musical gift.

The lesson was over and we were going to tea at the Century Plaza hotel. As Carrie went to gather her things, Irene quietly said to me, "Her voice is a gorgeous instrument." I saved the words to tell Carrie later.

Irene, concerned that it might rain, went into her bedroom and came out wearing a hat she bought in Vancouver.
She looked impish, put on her ultra suede jacket, grabbed her
purse, and we piled into Carrie's small car.

As soon as we pulled up to the hotel, Irene commented on
the excellent service, on the quality of the tea. We were served
with exquisite tea, little sandwiches, scones with clotted cream
and lovely jams. By the time the petit fours arrived, all we could
do was sip the second cup of tea.

With her cup of tea on the table, Irene put her arms out to
Carrie and said, "Tell a story when you sing. Forget that you
are a singer. It is the story that people hear."

"I have a story to tell," I said. And I recounted the story of
Carrie's battle with cancer.

Carrie interrupted, "Let me finish Mom." She spoke of the
time she had a laryngoscopy. "That was painful. Even though
they numb your nose, they put this flexible narrow tubing, like
thin spaghetti down your nose, through your throat and the
image of your vocal chords appear on the screen. The image was
clear, one vocal chord vibrated as I spoke. The other did not."

It was the first time I heard my daughter speak of pain.

Irene had her hand over her mouth.

"Carrie's doctor, Philomena McAndrews, told me that her
voice would probably never come back, but after the treatment,
after the surgeries, after the chemotherapy, and the radiation,
they could try injecting her damaged vocal chord with teflon."

Irene breathed the word, "Teflon?"

Carrie led Irene away from the horror and said, "Dr. Thompson, the radiologist said in his thirty years of practice he only heard a voice come back once, that of an elderly man."

"The story ends well, Irene. As you can hear Carrie can sing". .

Carrie took Irene's hands in hers and said, "I made a pact with God, that if I ever got my voice back, I would train it."

Irene Humphrey nodded her head, a silent tribute to Carrie's determination. Carrie's life force shone through and touched everyone with whom she came in contact.

It was the Passover season, the time of spring renewal.

The Letter "S"

SAFETY

All women, me included, need safety. What constitutes safety for women? For me, first and foremost, it is financial security. Our fast paced society continues to go faster and faster and is more and more demanding, depleting our resources in the quest for more and more: a house to live in, an apartment to rent or own, material possessions that shout at us from every venue from daily newspaper to the television commercials, luring us with desire, the newest technology, schools for our children, retirement for ourselves. And of course, overwhelming insurance bills plague us, from health insurance, to car insurance, to home insurance. Not to mention the last bills - funeral expenses - the list in between seemingly endless.

What is so obvious is often neglected by women be they young single women, single mothers, married women with families, divorced women or widows. Money in some circles is a taboo subject. But money needs to be out in the open. The struggle for financial equality in the workplace is ongoing. I am not a financial expert, nor one to give advice, but I do say, *save, save, save,* at least ten percent, and better yet twenty percent, whenever possible of any income you receive, *in your own name*. Sounds tough. It is! Money saved is a life cushion, a piggy bank, if you will, that can be dipped into for unusual expenses, a necessary vacation or entertainment time, for something in the future that is yet unnamed.

Above all, all women require a marketable skill. I repeat the phrase, a *marketable skill*. A diploma or a degree in hand is but a beginning. There must be a saleable skill: computer expertise, deep sea diving for marine research, teaching experience, stock market internship at a financial firm, draftsmanship, an architect's degree, a pilot's license. The list here is endless too. The days when women depended upon men for sustenance are long gone.

In order to survive with continually rising prices, many families now need two incomes: Husband and wife both are out in the work force, providing for their children, themselves, and in some cases, for their elderly parents. Fifty percent of marriages end in divorce, and if the women are dependent women, they often wind up without sufficient funds to maintain their previous life style. In a word, they are poor. And their children are poor.

When I was divorced my ex-husband, alimony and child support payments stopped – without rhyme or reason - after one year. I had to care for my two young children and had difficult choices to make. I always bought them new shoes. Their clothes, as they grew, were the best I could find at the Salvation Army store. I boiled some after bringing them home: Washing in soap and water, somehow, didn't seem adequate. My teacher's salary didn't quite make it to the end of the month. I learned to make chopped beef in ways that were imaginative, perhaps delicious, but to this day, I cannot look at a hamburger or ground meat in any form.

In time, I went to court and received a judgment for the payments. The order was good for twenty years. I never collected a dime. I rarely saw him. My ex-husband and his new wife lived in California, and then moved to Leonia, New Jersey with their baby boy several years later. He did see our children from time to time, but not me. The children would meet him in the lobby of the apartment building where we lived. On occasion I would see his back as he left the building from my apartment window. Although today's laws do demand child support, it is best to save, save, save, even in a good marriage. Save in your own name. It is now a felony offense not to pay child and it is about time.

My Aunt Anna, my father's sister, advised me to always have a '*knippel*', a Yiddish word that for me denoted cash tied up in a white handkerchief. No one, particularly husbands, knew about it and that money had to be stashed in a deep hiding place, preferably one's bra if the sum was not too great. This was the money saved by a wife out of the household funds to be spent as she wished: a gift for one of the children, a treat for herself or as an emergency fund for the household that had no bank account or savings.

I remember my paternal grandmother Lizzie Sidransky at

the end of her day selling buttons and thimbles from her push-cart on the Lower East Side, sitting down, raising her swollen feet on a chair, beckoning me to her and opening her wrinkled white handkerchief with great fanfare, pulling out a crushed dollar bill, handing it to me and saying, "Shh, this is for you. Save it. One day I will have another to give you and we will buy you a present."

She died when she was 58. Of hard work. Oh, there were medical terms I heard when I was an adult, but no matter. Life was difficult and she had seven children and an ailing husband to feed. Her body simply wore out.

Safety comes in many guises. I found that out when I was living in Europe. Pregnant with my second child, my husband was off in New York City, importing used Volkswagens from Germany, to create what I believed would be a financial safety net for our young family. He lived with his father who sent me $50 a month to live on. It was Spain, and money went farther than it did in the United States. His partner, the financier for the cars, remained in Spain. It was then, heavily pregnant, that I grappled with the financial vacuum that women find themselves in and it was then I resolved to never be dependent on anyone to sustain my financial life again.

I had to wait until I returned to the United States when I finally fulfilled my resolve to earn my own livelihood. I found a teaching position very near the apartment Saul rented for us in Riverdale. In the interim I returned to Spain, founded the American School of Barcelona, sued for divorce, and recreated my life, once more teaching in New York. All this detail is to reinforce the need for a solid education before setting off to begin an adult life, with all its pitfalls, joys, unexpected turns, illness, success, the gamut of life. I hark back to the Girl Scout motto I heard for the first time when I was ten years old: Be prepared.

Sounds so simple, but so critical, essential to the well being of a man, of a woman. We prepare boys for a working life, but not girls. Hopefully in the twenty-first century that is changing. We ask boys "What do you want to be when you grow up?" and do not ask, or did not ask the same question, of our female children with such intensity.

My father, who worked hard to support our family, said when I wanted to go to college, "Not necessary. Boys need the education, not girls as much." I was angered by his refusal to allow me to enter college without his blessing, but I went and worked part time in department stores. Menial jobs paid for my carfare, lunches and clothes. Books were free.

When I graduated with honors, my father beamed with pride and apologized saying, "I was wrong."

The Letter "T"

TRUST

The word 'trust' is bandied about often. One hears the word in arguments, in pleadings, in references to God. "In God we trust" is a motto we see on American coinage, on paper bills. Yet, I think of trusting yourself first, trusting your common sense, trusting your gut, your intuition, however you name that prickle of fine hairs on the back of your neck, the feeling in the pit of your stomach, a knowing that something is not quite right or is right on, before you offer trust to another human being. How do you trust yourself? How do you trust others? What is trust? Do you trust banks to keep your money safe? Do you trust your spouse to life long fidelity? Your friends? Your family? Do we ever regain the trust we had as children?

As children we trusted everyone although we were warned not to trust the smiling stranger who offered danger, rather than a treat. I trusted my mother's hand to hold me, to love me, to show me the way forward, be it to school, to the table for dinner, to a movie I would have to interpret for her, to the beginning of life. I trusted my teachers, some more than others. Trust is essential for surety, for the knowledge I can go forward, for the knowledge we can go forward. Trust was not yet firm in ourselves as children; we trusted the grownups in our lives, we trusted, sometimes in error. Yet we needed trust as children, and continue to need it into our entire lives, trust in ourselves, and in others.

For me, trust is knowing, above all, to trust myself, to allow myself to make a mistake, to trust myself to rectify that error. Some mistakes take longer than others to correct, if indeed, at all. I trust myself enough to feel that my endeavors will carry me through. Through what? The day. The week. The month.

There were goals I set for myself as a girl: not to fail my arithmetic test in the fifth grade (how I hated arithmetic), as a young woman about to strike out in the world, away from my parent's safe haven, (though in my case, that haven was fraught with imagined danger and fear), and as a middle aged woman, with a spouse and children. Now in age, I wonder if I can trust myself to live the end chapters with grace and face death with tranquility. Courage.

Trust is an elusive word, with different connotations for people. I trust that in crisis I will find someone or some institution that will see me through the hard days.

Trust is a process of connecting with yourself.

I search for the early days, the formative years when I dared to travel alone to Europe in my twenties, dared to take a bus to nowhere in Switzerland, away from yet another general strike in France. I packed my bag, went to the Paris bus station and got on the first one out of France, destination Lausanne, a

town, a city I had never heard of, not in the Bronx where I was
raised, or at Hunter College where I majored in history and
double minored in geography and economics. I knew only of
Geneva, the home of the League of Nations established after
World War I, and now the home of the United Nations, formed
after World War II to monitor the warlike behavior of so many
countries.

The bus was jammed and I was jammed into a seat next to
a rather large, or shall I say, very fat Frenchmen, whose bottom
more than inched over to my seat. I was young, I was slim,
so I squeezed my frame away from his protruding flesh, and
squeezed against the windowpane, watching the undulating
landscape as the bus drove on. And the bus stopped, Lausanne!
My ticket was to Lausanne.

With trepidation, I stepped off with my small suitcase into
a triangular parkette. Descending passengers quickly scattered
away and I sat on the single bench with nowhere to go. Then I
remembered, it was Friday, an early July evening. The Sabbath.
Surely there'd be a synagogue in this tourist city; surely I'd find
a room to sleep the night. I'd worry about tomorrow, tomorrow.
I hailed a cab and in my best high school French, I asked the
driver to take me to the nearest synagogue. Did I know where
it was? Did I know the name of the synagogue? Of course not.
I asked for the nearest one. I had no Swiss francs, only French
francs (the days before the 'euro') and green dollars. I tried to
explain. The driver shook his head, drove off and within minutes I was on the steps of the synagogue. It was too early for

services, but I was weary and concerned for my safety. I entered, sat in the back row and closed my eyes.

A small white haired man coughed softly and I opened my eyes. He asked, " Etes-vous jud?" Are you Jewish?

"Oui. Do you speak English?"

He answered with a question, "Do you understand Yiddish?"

"No," I said. How was I to explain to him that my mother tongue resided in my hands? Too complicated.

The questioning continued, and when he was satisfied with my request he offered me a nap on the back row, a place to rest until services began.

He left me with a final sentence. "I will find you a room with a family tonight."

Relieved, I fell asleep.

I awakened when a middle-aged woman gently tapped me on the shoulder. Services were about to begin. I sat up, removed my small backpack from the seat, and tucked it under my legs. A hush fell over the congregants. They'd finished their greetings, one to another. I was still, grateful to be among my own. People I'd never met, yet, felt deeply connected to.

Seeing the rabbi on the bima, watching the velvet clothed Torah scroll passed around the congregation for a moment's touch with the corner of the Bible, gave me a sense of home. And when the service was over, the small white haired man waited for me as I entered the aisle behind the others and introduced me to Frau B, a recent widow who had a spare room. Both of them ushered me to the community room where we took a bit of Sabbath wine, a bit of Sabbath bread, a challah passed around. I remember a few questions: "You are American?" "Here alone?" Why did you leave Paris?" Questions faded to concern. "You must be tired. Come, we shall go home. My daughter is just here." Her pretty blonde daughter was 10 years old.

The evening was dark, clouds hid the stars and I felt comfortable. Once in the apartment, Frau B bustled about the spare room, fluffing pillows on the narrow bed, and inviting me into the room to sleep. In the morning, I smelled hot chocolate and warm croissants. I seemed to float into her immaculate white kitchen.

After breakfast, Frau B said in heavily accented English, "Now we must find you a room in a pension where you can live for a few days until the French strike is over and you can return to your husband." I did not tell her at that moment I was quite unsure of ever finding Saul. The feeling passed.

The pension was clean, within walking distance of Lac Lehman, a beautiful lake. Days to myself, days to write. Would I ever be able to find my young husband working in Paris? He was staying at the Georges V hotel, and said he would leave Paris as soon as he could and that I should check the American Express offices in Geneva and in Lausanne. We would find each other one day or the next. There was no message for me in Lausanne, perhaps it was in Geneva. So I walked to the lake, sat on a bench and allowed the afternoon to pass without any anxiety, enjoying the summer day, the children at play, the older retirees strolling, lovers arm in arm and I was content until my stomach gurgled. Dinner time.

I sat alone at the pension table, ordered white wine, a filet of sole and I had something I'd never tasted before, creamed baked celery. My white plate was filled with delicious white food. I spoke with no one save the waitress. I was alone and it was good.

A group of young Lebanese men who were staying at the pension arrived for their dinner. One of the men, Ahmed, sallied over to my table, introduced himself, looked me over, smiled and made flirtatious comments. I was uncomfortable. I went to my room and moved the dresser to the door, blocking any entrance. Surely I was over reacting. Within half an hour, I heard men speaking Arabic outside my door. There was a gentle knock. I did not respond. The pounding began after one of the five men attempted to force the door. Then the shouting. I cowered, but did not move and did not make a sound. Fifteen minutes passed. They left. I had responded to that part of me aware of my intuition. I had responded to that part of me that had trust enough in myself to take action, minimal as it was. I was young yet I had the confidence instilled in me by my mother whose hands I can see now, signing, "Trust yourself."

Thousands of miles away and she was still protecting me. She'd understood the importance of repetition with young children. She'd sign, "You must teach children, and you must train them. Tell the lesson again and again." Her syntax was usually off, but her meaning was clear.

The Letter "U"

UNDERSTANDING

What do we understand about ourselves and our life paths? Yes, path is written in the plural. Most women have had several life paths, beginning with birth and ending, finally, in that great divide we name death. When I reflect on my own life, when I reflect on understanding who I was, and who I am today, I am overwhelmed with fragmentary memories, wondering if my memories create the understanding of the self.

There is an ecstasy to understanding; there is the aha moment of sudden comprehension of a difficult concept, of a mathematical formula, of an unexpected musical notation, of the mastery of yet another technical innovation connecting us, me and you, to all the corners of the world. That is one kind of understanding. I reflect on another kind of understanding: Self-understanding.

Did I understand myself as a young woman, as an inexperienced teacher, as a young mother? I think not. I was sucked into the path and walked into another phase of my life without any awareness of who I was. The task instead was to do the work. Teaching my first class as a regular, and not a daily substitute, in an all girls' Harlem school in mid-century was terrifying. As I left the Lenox Avenue subway station each morning before 8 AM, I breathed deeply and mentally prepared myself for the onslaught of teaching girls near my own age. These were girls of the slums, these were girls who were street smart, these were girls who passed notes to one another, surreptitiously they believed, until I could no longer tolerate the disruption, and seized one of these crumpled bits of yellow paper and read, "Meet me in the closet, we can hump there." In my naïveté, I had no inkling of what the note meant. The principal of the school grinned at me when she read the note and carefully explained the sexual reference. I was mortified.

I did not understand myself or the culture of these young girls of the Harlem slum. I had only a bare inkling of their lives when I made a home visit and met a 28 year-old mother of a 15 year-old girl in my class. Who had time to understand my own life path when the young girls I taught were so far away from my norm?

I had heard of teen-age pregnancy, but I had never encountered it face to face as I did with Gwendolyn's mother, who demanded that I keep a strong eye for her scrawny awkward daughter, lest she too suffered her mother's fate of early pregnancy and a life tied to welfare. I had not the experience to deal with this social dilemma, which is ongoing to this day, among black and white girls. Eventually I fled.

I was a young married, still a student, studying for an advanced degree in education. In time I did discover that I had other talents, other capacities, and did not want to teach full time in the New York City public school system. For me, it was a dead end, going nowhere, except to a pension after 30 or 35 years. I understood enough to leave and find another mountain to climb, another country to traverse, another language to speak. I had a young husband who shared these dreams. Away we went.

I was gifted with the capacity to understand languages without knowing the meaning of a particular word. If the sentence made sense, I got the gist. That gift, arising out of silence and parental deafness, carried me with pleasure in the years that followed in Europe, first as a traveler, and then as a resident of Vienna, Munich, Torremolinos and Barcelona.

Who had time to understand? I only had time to live and to discover. I wanted to understand new languages; I wanted to be immersed in new cultures; I wanted to have enough funds to continue the exploration of other places and other faces. Central Europe was freezing cold in the winter. I spent my energies staying warm.

I did not understand that I belonged to that generation of women who followed in their husband's footsteps, marching closely behind. Some of us followed with trepidation, others resentfully, others with absolute consent. I consented. I worked when I could to supplement our meager income, I wrote on a portable Royal typewriter that has now found its way into total obsolescence. I shopped in the local markets and learned how to say cheese, milk and meat in a foreign tongue. I followed the man, willingly. It was my choice. I chose to teach in Vienna, I chose, although asked, to be the founding director of the American School of Barcelona. Yes, I would teach for most of my life, here and there, different subjects in different places. If I could read it and understand it, I could teach it. Whatever that 'it' was. Perhaps it was the gift of my parent's insatiable curiosity who taught me unknowingly how to teach and how to think.

Then a child was born. My first, a girl, a little wizened thing who grew to be a great beauty and a light to everyone in her path. Did she understand who she was before her early death? I doubt she gave it a thought. She was too busy trying to conquer cancer and stay alive for her children. She clung to her role as a mother. Before she had her children, I was mother, mother above all, to my own. We who are mothers, who share the love of our children, in our own ways, do share a common bond of understanding, the understanding of motherhood. Each culture presented another facet of motherhood to me.

When I proudly wheeled Carrie in her carriage, with our brindle boxer in tow, stout German women would stop to ogle the dog, and then the baby and remark on how thin she was, advising me to put flour in her milk to fatten her up. I smiled, thanked them, and was horrified at the unsolicited advice. I moved on, to the sunshine, to a stroll in the English Garden, so beautiful in the spring, the air warmer now, and I was, I believe, happy. Did I stop to reflect? No. I enjoyed the moment.

Dr. Spock, the famed pediatrician, and I raised Carrie together. His work still holds, his common sense appealed to my sensibilities. There was no one else there to advise me. My mother was half a continent and an ocean away from my daily life in Munich, Germany. I remember my mother's words to me, words that indicated that I would be the best judge of my own life, to trust my intuition. I had no choice. I could not, nor would I, accept the martinet discipline engendered by German child rearing philosophy. It may not have been a national trait, but that is the advice I received from those around me.

When my son Mark was born in Barcelona three years later, the Spanish sensibility was totally different. In the park where mothers and nannies gathered in the Mediterranean sunlight, so many boys were called, "*Rey*". Did they all have the same name? No, *rey* means king. Every male child was a king. And *reina,* Spanish for queen, was the name of every female child. How delightful to be so regarded by adults.

Inherent in those endearing names is respect, cordiality and dignity for every child. Children who were not of school age went to bed at the same time as their parents, sometimes as late as midnight. They were part of the family immediately. For me the most wondrous trait in rearing babies was not to allow them to cry. As soon as a cry was heard, someone went to pick up the baby, to let the baby know that he or she was not alone, to offer comfort, to check on a need for the child. Raising Mark and Carrie in Barcelona was a nourishing part of my life.

My husband was out cavorting with other women, sleeping with other women, that he probably met in the bar in which he was some kind of partner in the Barrio Chino. I was totally oblivious (or so I thought) to his wanderings, so busy was I with my children and the running of my Spanish household. Before our divorce that took place in California, he confessed his sexual prowess in such a gross manner that I chased him out of the house with a boiling pot of water. I will never know if I would have actually thrown it at him. His escape from my shock and wrath was swift.

Did I understand? I don't know. What was there to understand? Him, or me. The constant movement from city to city, from language to language, absorbed so much of my time, that I cocooned myself into my own life orbit. My primary understanding was that of being a mother. Self-reflection? There was no time for such frivolity.

I had to leave the San Francisco area where we located after our move from Spain. Once more, I found myself in New York; I had to earn a living, to support myself and my children. I could not move out of my mother and father's Queen's one bedroom apartment until I found work. I worked for the Board of Education, something I swore I would never do again. Yet, circumstance and money determined my immediate future. There was no choice, there was doing, and I did.

I taught in Queens, I worked as a Non-English coordinator, giving demonstration classes with South American boys far too old to be enrolled in junior high school in Brooklyn. I taught briefly as an instructor at Hunter College in New York. It tickled my fancy when I was told to leave the faculty elevator, that I was a student avoiding the crowded student elevators.

"I am faculty," I insisted.

That remark was greeted with a sneer by every elevator operator until a professor vouched for me saying, "Yes, she is new and she is faculty."

That was fun.

Moves from one country to another continued. I met a Canadian, a divorced man, Richard, who was in the film business, intelligent, and he offered me and my children home and hearth in Toronto. Suburbia indeed. I longed for a settled life, a place of permanence for us. I soon found that suburbia and I were not suited.

My constant companion was one that Betty Friedan in her book the FEMININE MYSTIQUE predicted: a vacuum cleaner. Tongue in cheek, of course. Or perhaps not. But I was lonely stuck in a lovely house, with a spacious backyard and a two car garage and a husband who appeared every night asking, "What's for dinner?" My children were displaced, never quite finding a place for themselves growing up. They were the foreigners, the Americans. I did not know it then, but foreigners, particularly Americans, were not looked upon with the greatest of favor.

It was then, in my late thirties and early forties, when I began a serious study of my life. Did I know what I was doing? Did I understand my motivations? Or was I swept up in the never-ending stream of what was expected of a young mother, a divorced woman with two wonderful children?

In Canada, I first met overt anti-Semitism. Central Europe,

particularly Vienna, was a cauldron of suppressed anti-Semitism after World War II. Survivors of the Nazi industrial murder of Jews - many who returned for reparations or for medical treatment to German cities were cared for by the German government. I knew some of these people. My maternal family of 60 was murdered, including my maternal great grandparents. There were two survivors, two women who have disappeared into other lands. I did not expect any anti-Semitism in Toronto, not among a North American citizenry of almost two million people. When I moved there, the estimated number of Jews in the city was about 250,000 and bit by bit, I was introduced to the underlying WASP anti-Semitism.

Leaving the vacuum cleaner to the broom closet, I found my way to a museum, the Art Gallery of Toronto. I became a docent, and as someone said to me later, I was one of the token Jews at the museum. I ignored the remark. I became friendly with a woman, Diana G., who eventually held the reins of the Women's Committee as President, a powerful group involved with funding the museum. Each year, she and her husband, a Toronto FFT (First Family of Toronto) gave a rousing party for all connected with the museum. She played the drums, her husband jazz on their grand piano. For several years running, Richard and I attended this fun bash at their home, not too far from our home. One year, the invitation arrived in the mail and I picked up the phone to respond immediately and said, "Richard will be out of town on business, but I will come alone." There was silence at the other end of the line, some mild coughing, a dog barking, a child shouting, and she said, "I'll call you back." It was a household in a moment of chaos.

Ten minutes later the phone rang. And she said, "I cannot have a Jewess alone at my party."

Without a word, I place the receiver on the cradle and never spoke to her again.

What on earth was I doing? Why had I befriended this woman who ate at my table, whose children played with my children, whose interests and mine were compatible? So I thought. I should have been clued in, but I was so caught up in the river of suburban life, trying to fit in, trying to avoid that vacuum cleaner, that I ignored more than one obvious sign. Richard and I had dinner with a business acquaintance and this man, Waring C, said, "This is the first time I have eaten with a Jew." I gasped internally, made a flip remark, and treated the rest of the evening lightly. After all, this was not Germany.

The year before I was refused admission to my friend Diana's party, we went as a group of several couples to Mexico where the men had business interests in a silver mine in Guanajuato, the center of Mexican silver mining. I was elected as the sole Spanish speaker to herd the women to restaurants and to shopping areas. I accepted the role as chaperone to these well-dressed, well-heeled women around Mexico City. Anything to leave the broom closet behind. When we all finally convened in Puerta Vallarta, a resort town, we celebrated a successful trip at a piano bar. There was music and there was dancing and general good feeling.

One of the men, Larry G. asked me to dance, and once on the floor he said, "I never danced with an earthy Jewess before."

I laughed off the remark.

How could I have been so stupid, so naïve?

I was at my physical prime in my early forties and I had not given credence to the innuendos blatantly said to my face. What was said behind my back? What was said after 5 PM when men and women in the privacy of their living rooms, cocktails in hand, made anti-Semitic remarks within earshot of their children?

I spoke with Rabbi Gunther Plaut of Holy Blossom Temple in Toronto about this flagrant anti-Semitic behavior. He was a learned rabbi, a German Jew, a man of wisdom, who fled Nazi Germany, a loving man whom everyone respected. He treated me gently and said, "You have to recognize the five o'clock shadow that exists in Canada. Jews are not socially welcome after business hours."

Later, I read a book by two Canadians, Abella and Troper, NONE IS TOO MANY, a book whose title is attributed to a remark made by an unidentified immigration officer when asked about the policy of admitting Jews to Canada. He said, "None is too many." William Lyon MacKenzie King was the prime minister during this time and he supported this policy of exclusion by the head of Canadian immigration. From 1933-1948, Canada admitted only 5000 Jews, the lowest number of any Western country. Jewish refugees from concentration camps, from work camps, from hidden places in forests and sewers, were not wanted.

It was time to leave. I wanted to return home to the United States. Yes, there was racism of many kinds, but not the hidden kind of our Canadian neighbor. I did not expect this of the Canadian people. I was deeply troubled.

In order to understand myself, I had to understand *the world politic* in which I was living, in which I was raising my children. What was there to understand? I wanted change: It was a rare moment of assertion for me. I wanted out of Canada, where I could not make headway into the society at large and had to live behind imaginary ghetto walls established by the establishment. I did not deal with this in Spain; I chose to blindly exclude myself from the body politic in the aftermath of World War II in Germany and Austria. I survived as a declared Jew during my years in these countries.

I understood that the world was complex, and I could only try to understand myself and those close to me. If anyone had to be rescued from following the 'man' it was me. Yet, Richard, ever the entrepreneur, agreed to the change, and we decided to be gone from Canada for two or three years at most.

We never left the United States. Richard died here and was buried in Florida. I had been living a realized life and did not recognize it as such. Each decade, each experience had its own realization. I had to stop and breathe and reflect to know myself, to know that each phase of my life contributed to understanding who I was and who I might become, but that was down the yellow brick road. I had but to put on my red shoes and follow the path that said, "Come, this is life."

Tikkun Olam is a Hebrew phrase that says *heal the universe*, goes on to say, *one person at a time*. Healing and understanding were beginning to come together as a life move, a patterning of my life. I was beginning to understand. I know I will never completely understand and I am in my ninth decade. Some say it takes a lifetime to understand. Understanding is a continuum, if we bother; it is never ending, for all the days of my life, of our lives.

My question is, then, what is it I wish, we wish, to understand?

The Letter "V"

VALOUR

There are many, many women who lead unsung lives of valor. My mother was one. My daughter another. There are very few women who made the pages of history with their incredible feats, women of the Bible, Rachel and Esther, women of war, Joan of Arc, women of politics, Margaret Thatcher, the conservative prime minister of the United Kingdom from 1979-1990, women who stood behind men and were their legs and arms. Eleanor Roosevelt was incredible. She traveled and spoke during her husband Franklin Delano Roosevelt terms in office, from 1933 until his death in 1945. And there is the famed Nobel Peace Prize winner, Mother Teresa who devoted her life caring for the poor in India until she died in 1997. There are others: Sally Ride, the first woman astronaut in space, or Hannah Senesch, a 23 year old Jewish resistance fighter who parachuted behind enemy lines during WWII, was captured by the Nazis and executed. These are women whose names are indelible. The list goes on.

There are so many whose names are not indelibly etched in time's passage, yet they are women we all know, we have all met at one time or another: a school teacher left her mark on our psyches, a beloved aunt, a friend, a woman with whom we had a chance meeting who left us with a story, or lesson learned.

In the years we lived in Munich, I met several survivors, men and women who were trying to reassemble their upside-down lives. I remember Nellie A., a survivor of the Holocaust, mauled with medical experiments in one concentration camp after another, who tried over and over to have a baby, a baby to remember her dead, a baby to go on living. She had spontaneous natural abortion after spontaneous natural abortion. Nellie was round and warm, blonde and loving. I marveled at her sweetness, her zest for life after the years at Auschwitz. She was strong enough to survive the Death March, in January 1945, when so many evacuees dropped in the snow and were summarily shot to death by the retreating Nazis. Nellie was a survivor who carried hope for the next generation.

There was Irene B. who gave birth to Ava. Irene was a philosophy professor who lived out the war in plain sight as a Catholic in Warsaw. She was old, her face frayed with lines beyond her actual years, but her body somehow kept her reproductive organs intact. She went hungry during the war, but she did not starve, perhaps becoming the saving grace for another generation. After the war, she met and married a man, several years younger than she was; his wife and two young sons were murdered by the Nazis.

She and her husband married for one reason, to have a child, to defy Hitler's Final Solution, his promise that every Jew would be eradicated from the earth's surface. Her baby Ava was exquisite, with dark, dark curly hair, huge black eyes and a gentle smile. I liked Irene from our first meeting. We became good friends in the way of mothers who wheel their baby carriages in the spring sunshine. What happened to Irene and Ava after her frail husband died of tuberculosis, I do not know. I do know that I shall always remember her insistence on keeping part of the Jewish gene pool alive, albeit only hers and her young husband's. I will remember her intensity. I will remember her courage, day by day, working under the Nazi aegis, speaking Polish without a trace of a Yiddish accent. Her language that kept her alive after all the members of her family were killed.

Then I met Esther. She never menstruated after spending her teen years in the forest. She too was incapable of bearing a child of her own body. She never conquered the English language, and try she did. She was thirty years old when I met her for the first time. She was a survivor, the wife of a survivor, who like my student Clara, never had a home of her own. She and her husband kept renting one Nazi widow's room after another, always on the move. I suspect they had diamonds sewn in the lining of their winter coats. They did have to flee once more.

I spent time with these women. We had innumerable cups of coffee, sometimes we had dinner, something that was called, *abend brot*, evening bread, a meal more akin to our lunch. We broke bread together and never discussed our Jewish heritage. I did not ask, I did not comment. I accepted the terms of their survival after the war ended. They were my European family.

And when we left Munich for Barcelona, I never heard from them or spoke with them again.

Women of valor, who continued living, who continued giving, for that was the purpose of life, their individual lives, after so much murder in the name of the purification of the Aryan/German population under Adolph Hitler's Nazi regime. To live was enough.

These were vibrant women, in their late twenties or early thirties; these were the ones who had the health and physical stamina to withstand the onslaught of Nazi horror. These are extreme cases of women of valor. There are women of valor too, women who do not mark the pages of history, but who enhance the lives of their families.

One such woman was my mother, Mary, a name given to her by a Trenton schoolteacher who did not approve of her Hebrew name: Miriam Shifra Bromberg.

There are no words I can write or say that could possibly convey the nuance of life expressed in her long slender fingers. She was my mother, surely, but she enchanted all the children who came under her flirtatious spell. There was no artifice, no guile, just pure glee in the presence of small children. They got her immediately, a connection so rare that to experience it was a life gift. She knew how to play with them and they loved her. I loved her. She was mine. Or as my oldest granddaughter would say, she was *mines*. Always in the plural.

My mother is gone these many years now, yet I can see her standing before me, advising me to take the right step even if is out of step of the norm. She didn't know the words that I write as a sentence, but she knew when to strike out, when to be that maverick woman, the woman who dared to be different from the others. She gave me up to my husband, and I had no understanding then what a loss it was for her. She lost her voice, me. She had said, "First you train your children, then you teach them, and then you let them go. They will always come home." These are not her signed words, but close enough to her intent, to her extraordinary wisdom and strength I feel free writing them. Rather than an exact word for word translation from American Sign Language, it is a clear interpretation of her meaning.

I think of my grandmother Lizzie Sidransky who braved the seasons standing in front of a pushcart selling sundries to feed her seven children and ill husband. I think of my grandmother Fanny who lived alone in London, in a small apartment with ten others for the better part of three years, waiting for her husband to send money for passage to the Golden Land, the United States of America. Women of valor.

A woman of valor has been interpreted as a reference to the Divine Presence, to the Sabbath, to wisdom and the soul. Although each life's trajectory is different, there is a common denominator, that of an internal feminine presence, a presence that all women know without any explanation.

When I was strolling the hills of the island of Corfu, in Greece on a balmy summer's morning, I stopped in front of a small white washed house to admire creamy roses that were the sizes of small heads of cabbage. My husband and friends walked on and I said, "Go on ahead, I'll catch up."

The door opened and a tiny woman walked out and she and I started a lengthy conversation about her children, her life as a widow, her cataracts and her flowers. We chatted and gesticulated for about ten minutes until my husband and friends waved to me in a motion that said, "come and join us". I bid this woman goodbye, and she cut an enormous rose to give me. I accepted with gratitude.

When I reached my husband he said, "What was that all about?" I told him what the tiny lady and I discussed. He said, "Ruth, I didn't know that you speak Greek."

"I do not speak Greek, not a word, not thank you, not good morning."

Grace most certainly. Valor most probably.

There is mystery to living day by day. To this day I know we communicated, that we understood each other's story, but neither of us had any idea of the other's spoken language, not Greek, not English. I have no explanation. We were connected women.

I think of the women who crossed the territories of the West, with their men and cattle and hope and seeds for planting in the 18th and 19th century. Did they have any inkling they would be known not by name, but revered as women who helped create the United States from sea to sea? No. If I search my imagination, if I trust my intuition, I see these women of value struggling with life itself as they made the crossing in covered wagons, braving heat and cold, braving their own doubts as to why they were making this impossible journey. Yet, they persevered with their men and their children to find another life, another place to settle, a place of safety, a place of prosperity.

We who seek out another way to live do usually create another world, if only for ourselves. We may be wounded, scarred in the process, but we continue with the most precious of gifts, life.

The Letter "W"

WOUNDS WORDS WISDOM

Wounds, words and wisdom, are the words that spring to mind as I write this. We are all subject to life's wounds, physical and emotional. Words do not necessarily ease those wounds. It took a long time for me to recover from the betrayal of my first marriage, to suffer the indignity of being left behind for a younger woman, a mere secretary, such a banal ending to what I believed was an exciting marriage. Abandonment is not easy. No words will erase the pain I felt, the pain my children felt and our dislocation, geographically and mentally.

Then, there is the wisdom that time promises. It does not always arrive. For me, wisdom is the capacity to cope with adversity, and when the adversity occurs I hope I am wise enough to recognize the dilemma and not look the other way into the maw of destructive denial. Wounds leave scars, some greater than others, and the cliché holds: time does heal many wounds. But how did I deal with the terror of being alone with two young children, no income, no job, and no place to live? I did. I found my way home to my mother and she was instrumental in healing my open sore.

"Keep busy," she said "and I will see to the children." And she did. Then began the question of 'self'. Who was I without a male anchor?

"Who am I?" was the question so many of us beg for an answer.

We, in our Freudian Christian American society, speak quite often of our early childhood years, the formative years, the molding time, but how much attention do we pay to the early adult years, to our twenties and thirties where we lay down the patterns of adult living? How did those years shape us, shape me for the decades that followed, to my forties and fifties, sixties and seventies?

When I was in my early sixties, I struggled with the question that had, in the end, no definitive answer. I asked this:

Who was that young woman who bore two children in foreign countries, who smuggled goods for Holocaust survivors? Who was the woman who, in the mid-fifties, when my contemporaries were climbing the social and economic ladder, living in homes of their own, pressed like trees to suburban life, rooted to the dream of acquisition: weekends at golf clubs, wielding a sports weapon, a golf stick, a tennis racket. People who later surgically lifted their faces in search of eternal youth, capped their teeth, compared their coronary bypasses waiting for the end of days reveling in their children and grandchildren (the lucky ones) and hoping when death comes it is swift and no one suffers? Who was that woman

who chose another path, a different way to live life? Who
was that woman who was nearly smothered in suburban
Toronto? Was she yet woman? Was she a child? Do the for-
mative years exist in each decade of life?

Questions, questions and no clear answers.

And when do our wishes enter the equation? Do we stop
wishing for things, for experiences, for love, for a vacation, for
another house, another apartment, another city in which to
live? How about Paris? Or New York? Some farm in Montana?

Each decade brings us closer to death. We humans enter, if
we are gifted, endowed with the spirit of living, an entry into
newness once more, each birthday, each year a new beginning,
a promise of life. The ultimate human endeavor, the ultimate
gift of life is life itself. It is the next sunrise, and the next, and
the next.

It is not avoidance of death, nor fear of death, for death must
have its own comfort. No, it is the celebration of life itself, be
it a sad day or a joyous one, be it painful or glorious or a blessedly ordinary one. As we Jews often toast one another with the
words, *L'Chaim, To Life* I write once again, *life is the treasure.*

So as I sit here typing on this gray day, I salute life. But I still
ask, "Who was twenty-year-old me?" Who was that abandoned
woman? Who was that woman who remarried and moved once
more to a foreign country? Who is that older woman I have
become? Perhaps it matters not. Perhaps the questions have no
validity. Perhaps who I am, perhaps who we are, changes from

day to day, from week to week, and from year to year, until we finally become who we are, fluid in personality, in dreams and in actions.

I am many. Child. Daughter. Student. Teacher. Wife. Mother. Smuggler. Divorcee. Writer. Grandmother. This is the mechanical sum, but not the sum of my parts.

I need the centering calm of solitude. A day of silence, a day of restoration, away from the madness of the clamoring 'others', of their needs and desires, of their warmth and humanity. A day for me, a day for the self. A day to watch God's treat: my new orchid, a veined violet Vanda, unfold into full flower so perfect, so beautiful, its central slipper, deep tongued and voluptuous. A day to drive in the blaze of New England autumn, leaves of vibrant color, a canopy testifying to life's majesty shot through with unexpected brilliant sunshine that stops motorists on the road, who sit and stare at this wondrous changing of the guard, from summer to fall, from fall, finally to the purity of winter's snow. We drive on, usually at a slower speed.

All this quiet is placed into an emotional bank account, solitude accumulated, soul sweetened, and 'self' present. It is in the stillness of silence that I am yet another me. And all the parts of me are who I am, as good a summation as any. All the parts of me, at some level change daily. No one is static. Life is not static.

Life arrives in pieces and continues in a broken line. Fragmented for most women. Certainly for me. Although I would like life to be one simple line I could follow without digression, it is not so. I do not wish life to be fragmented. I do not wish to deal with all the threads that pop up unexpectedly out of life's cloth. Once I believed life's pieces could be organized: some discarded, some heeded, some cherished. This is not so. I think of my English friends who, when in distress offered the phrase, "Oh, do get on with it." Whatever that 'it' was.

Now in my eighties as I type away, hopefully with wisdom gained through living, and dying, I know without a doubt, that wisdom comes in many guises, that wisdom changes from experience to experience, that wisdom exists not only in our beings, but in our daily choices, in a life style that promises health and joy. I have seen enough of death, the death of those I loved and continue to love. It is time to live. It seems as though I have inherited the lives of those lost to me, the bits and pieces that were unfinished. But I cannot finish the life of another.

I cannot finish my own life. It is an ongoing process.

The Letter "X"

I have decided to let the letter X stand on its own. No anecdotes to tell. Unless I extend my resources to include other words with other beginnings: excellence, extraordinary, extra, but these stretch the alphabet beyond expectation. So, dear reader, I leave it to your fertile imaginations to write your own story.

The Letter "Y"

YELLOW

For Carrie

(*Who shone her beautiful light on everyone she touched*)

Yellow is the color of life.

Yellow is the color of the sun, warm and nurturing. Yellow dots meadows, weed dandelions popping their heads above the green grass, here, there, over yonder, under foot, heralding the longed for Northern spring. Ah yes, daffodils come up yellow every spring; the promise of renewal of the soil, of dancing heads in the gentle breeze. Up they come, little green spikes of color poking through exposed earth, brown, clay like. Yet, the heavy soil and the winter snows have kept the daffodil bulbs fed and safe. Here they are, sometimes in fields, an army of yellow fragrant flowers, sometimes sticking up in an urban patch of dirt. Oh, yes, the color of life.

I promised Carrie in the fall months before she died, she would see the daffodils come up yellow this spring. She did not. Although it is not the Jewish custom to bring flowers to a grave, I am tempted this fall to bury a few daffodil bulbs at her gravesite. Her soul would delight at the sight of fresh yellow blooms. Is it forbidden to plant flowers? Perhaps it is merely custom, tradition that we leave only stones on the tombstone, signaling our presence, our visit to the gravesite.

There are tulips that grace my table every spring. I push my cart through the local supermarket, head for the flowers, leave the hyacinths and the other forced blooms, and search for tight budded yellow tulips. I find them. Perfect. Which bunch do I choose? In pots or cut? One bud open, the rest closed and home they come with me. Now where to place the shock of yellow? On the kitchen table, in the patio, no matter, my house shines with yellow light, the light of the sun.

Yellow is the tight tufted prickly bloom crowning the plump barrel cactus in an Arizona desert. Gardens of succulents thrive in parched desert soil. Yet, the color yellow sprouts, yellow pokes up and says I live everywhere. I live on bird feathers. I am a canary, yellow. Some small finches have bright yellow feathers, their tiny bodies alive with yellow flame. Others have bright yellow feathers warming their black feathers. If we look, there is yellow.

Yellow is the color of light, creating a way through darkness. Yellow illumines our streets: lamplight, headlights, neon lights. At night, house lights in windows, in homes, in apartments suffuse the dark streets with yellow as I drive by, wondering about the lives lived within. I know nothing of the people who inhabit the lit spaces. I imagine, I make up stories; I am after all a writer. So I think: a good marriage, a bad marriage, children in bed, a lonely widower downing his third whiskey, a young girl living alone, straight out of college, degree in hand, facing lonely evening after lonely evening. I stop the wonder at lives lived behind the yellow glow of forced light and move on to my own incandescent series of lit rooms banishing the dark night.

And remember.

I remember the children when they were young. I remember the poem I taught them on a starlit night. *"Starlight, star bright, /First star I see tonight/ I wish I may, I wish I might/Have the wish I wish tonight."*

The rhyme hitches to a luminous yellow star. And how I wished upon that first star when I was a child, and sometimes mumble a wish under my breath even now. The wish, always a talisman of hope.

As a child, as a teen-ager, I lived in brick buildings on cracked concrete streets and when summer bloomed in nearby parks, shiny bright yellow buttercups lifted their heads to the sun, to the sky; I was filled with glee. I'd pick one, then two and clutch the flowers hidden in my small hands and one day, an old woman stopped me and said, "Leave them for others to enjoy." So I did. But the temptation was too great for my eight-year-old granddaughter. She picked flowers from the fields or from neighbor's gardens and handed them to me: bedraggled bouquets with the same glee I picked a single yellow buttercup from a scraggly city garden. Sarah indeed, Carrie's little girl, imbued with *zest*, now grown.

When Sarah was little she chased the clear yellow butterflies outside the summerhouse in Egremont. Oh what joy! She'd stand quietly, stick out her fist until one would alight on the back of her grimy child's hand. She was oh so still, no movement, lest she spoil the perfect equilibrium of the gorgeous butterfly and her lovely barely perceptible breath.

When the creature flew off she turned to me and in a hushed voice said, "Nana, did you see that?"

I smiled and in a hushed voice to match her delight, said, "Yes, I saw that".

As I write these words, Sarah's mother, my daughter Carrie is gone, gone to her eternal rest. How Carrie loved springtime, the season of Passover, when we cleaned and cooked for the holiday, when we boiled eggs hard with clear yellow yolks, for the Seder feast, when we dipped them in salt at the dinner table, heralding the yolk of life, the egg, the symbol of life. And in November, the month of Carrie's death, Rachel, my other granddaughter, lit 50 butter candles high in the mountains of Bhutan, commemorating Carrie's life with the 50 yellow flames.

Yellow is the color of hope. It is the memory of the past, the promise of tomorrow and all the tomorrows to come. And what is hope? The continuum of life ordinary, of life extraordinary. Hope!

Carrie relied on hope.

"It gives me hope", she said, a few days before her death "to be able to fire the hospice people" if she was to be endowed with the miracle of ongoing life.

It was not to be. Yet, she had hope, hope framed by warmth, by the sunlight that would never bathe her beautiful face again.

Hope surely, as long as we live, is to know that one day follows another and we go on hoping for ourselves, for our children, for our families, our friends, for our life orbit. Hope is, for most of us, a life force.

Summer passes into fall. The trees give up their leaves, once green and now aflame in their last burst of glory. On some trees in the northern climes, leaves turn yellow overnight, and when the morning sun shines its light upon the tree, their porous leaves become golden. In the yellow-gold of the tree is promised rest, the rest of the winter to come, the snow and the cold. The season of bright yellow is over. We wait once again for the sun to warm the soil, to warm our lives. Life springs forth season after season.

The Letter "Z"

ZEST

The letter 'z' ends the 26 letters of the alphabet. The letter 'z' is not often used in the English language but it contains a great word. Zest. Zest for life. The thrill of the day. The rise of the morning sun. To begin again and again in life's path, whatever that path may be.

There are beginnings and there are endings. I could not have survived the ending of my daughter's life, her last days, if not for my friends. Women's friendships at life's final pages are more than a blessing; they are a necessity for survival. They, my friends, imbued with a zest for life, passed it on to me, enjoined me to go on living and see the sunshine, walk in the sunshine. I inherited the days my daughter did not live, the hours she wanted. Perhaps I will live some of them for her. Her zest for life was powerful.

She was so angry during her illness, perhaps the anger kept her alive. In the last weeks, so frail, so fragile, so docile, so loving, fighting, fighting until the last breath for her life. She knew, somewhere, somehow that her life was ending, and all she wanted was to go on living an ordinary life. She was so thin, so ill, so eager to have her life continue.

"I just want to be normal Mom. Live a normal life."

Her life was unfinished.

Her son Ben said, "Mom will not dance at my wedding."

Sometimes life comes hurtling at me, sometimes I want the world to close the door, stop revolving around the sun and give me a minute to breathe alone, so I can forgive her anger fanned by the cancer that invaded her body, she was furious; she was losing the battle for her life.

The day before she died, she said, "I'm going to beat this."

From time to time, I give in to fatigue. I lie down on the couch and think of Carrie, see her, feel her, hear her voice. Hospitalized for most of the last two months of her life, she spent her days watching television cooking shows, planning her own cooking show for children with digestive issues. She was starving. She could not keep food down. Yet her passion was never compromised, her passion continued to the very last moments of her life as we, friends and family, circled her bed, held her hand and whispered words of love as she lay dying. She was Carrie, bold and brave.

I sat with her in death. I touched her face, cold, frozen in beauty, frozen in death's embrace, without pain creasing her forehead. She is safe now, out of harm's way.

Death and its aftermath does not come in neat little packages that we can store on a shelf, somewhere out of the way of our daily routine. Life continues. This includes pleasure in life. Zest for happiness, for contentment, for food, for the unexpected moment of glee. Grab life, hold on to it, enjoy it.

Know zest.

It is a great gift.

Epilogue

I have often said that we die in mid-sentence.

I have repeated a toast that I feel is apt when we are with friends, toasting each other with a glass of wine, or as some of us might now, toasting with a crystal glass of water, I say, "Live long, die fast." I do believe that every life is incomplete; every life is unfinished when the final breath is taken, when the life force is gone and we are committed to the deep, to the ground, to the fire or as in some cultures, to a twigged, logged altar for the vultures to pick us clean. Yet, there is always one more thing to do, to see, to say, to hear, to taste.

Life is a finite arc.

We are done. Life accomplished.

Rather than dwell on death, I turn my thoughts to life, to the life I have already lived and to the future, for however long or short it may be. Although my body tires easily, my mind is as active and supple, if not more so, than when I was a young woman burdened with 'womanly doings'. And so I say hail to those I love: to my family and to my friends. Hail to life! *L'Chaim!*

In the southwestern corner of Massachusetts where I live summer and fall, I love the early morning light when the winds are still. It is the time before the rising winds cast armloads of yellow and crimson leaves to the already littered lawns. Then when the wind rises and cascades of leaves announce their fall to the earth, announce the onset of the coming winter in one final burst of gorgeous color. So it is every year, the turning of the seasons, so beautiful in the Northeast. I see my father's hands circling one on top of the other in an attempt to reach the heavens, to explain to me when I was a little girl, not only the change of seasons, but the spiraling crescendo of life itself and its ultimate demise. So great was his eloquence, in one swirling gesture, his face squarely in mine, his hands saying, "Understand now?"

I didn't then.

I do now.

Immortality is the child's gift: Death is 'never'.

I think of my mother. I hearken back to my mother and her spool of thread. When I was a girl, my mother charged herself with the task of teaching me 'womanly arts;' a phrase that was not part of her deaf lexicon. As she aged into her late seventies, I wondered at the time left to her, to us. I can see her, head bent over her tin sewing box, selecting the right color thread to sew on a loose button, to hem a dress that was too long for me, and to truss a chicken she stuffed with savory bread and onions. I see her tortoise shell comb tucked neatly into her chignon, hiding her thinning hair. I've watched my mother sew silk lamp shades with stitches so fine that they were invisible. She'd pick up one of my father's worn socks from her sewing basket and she'd sign, "Life can be full of holes like old socks. We sew up the holes and we wear the socks." She'd smile her enigmatic smile. She was beautiful.

When I was seven or eight years old, (time dims exact memory) my mother said, "I'll teach you to thread a needle."

I wanted to play with my doll but she had other plans.

Rain pounded on the window pane. My mother distracted me by opening her tin enameled box decorated with a cream colored calla lily and in one motion, unwound a length of thread from a white spool, slid it steadily into the eye of her silvery needle, drew down two equal lengths and between her left thumb and forefinger fashioned a small knot.

"Now you do it."

At first the thread flopped before I could reach the eye of the needle. "Here, let me show you! " She put the tip of the white cotton canvas in my mouth. "Make it wet. It slides in easily." It did.

Years and years later when I visited her in Florida, she once again insisted on sewing a loose button on my white shirt. "Bring me my sewing box, in the bedroom, top dresser drawer, the one on the left."

She was left-handed. I am left-handed.

There it was; the tin box with the calla lily stamped on the dark brown enameled surface, the same candy box I remembered as a child, now filled with discarded buttons: leather buttons, mother-of-pearl buttons, tiny white shirt buttons, straight pins and safety pins, thin needles and large embroidery needles, and spools of thread of every color. And one new untouched spool of white thread.

In less than a minute, she threaded a needle, sewed on my button and handed me the new spool of thread. "It's good luck. When you were a little girl you had new notebooks for school with thick white clean paper. This is new white thread. When you need to be calm, sew!"

That single spool connects us.

She was powerful, particularly when she taught me with her hands. When I pressed forward with my daily routine of husband-home-children-career, she urged me to stay home on weekends and "sew something."

I shook my young woman's head at her, informing her with that single nod that I was too busy. I ignored her common sense plea for calm, for rest, for the rhythm of the plying needle: in-out. A meditative task.

That meditative task kept me sane when my grown daughter was treated for almost a year with chemotherapy and radiation for lymphoma. My mother, older now, sent me a needlepoint kit from New York's Metropolitan Museum of Art, a copy of a corner of a well-known medieval tapestry. As I sat in the 'chemo room' watching over my daughter as the IV poured medicines to destroy the cancer in her body, I sewed. I sewed mornings, afternoons and early evenings. As I watched her sleep, I sewed and sewed and prayed. The canvas was small, the stitching fine, and I had to pay attention, meditating on each stitch, on the colors of the wool, blotting out all thought. I blessed my mother for the lessons I learned at her hands.

She and I used our hands, worked with our hands, talked with our hands. Our messengers. The skills of woman's hands: healing skills, touching skills, knitting skills, sewing skills and language skills were exchanged by hand. She was nearly illiterate when she faced the printed page, but her hands were masterful teachers.

"Life," my mother said, "is a spool of thread." When I was young, I didn't quite understand her animated hands. But now, I know what she wanted to say. One draws thread from the spool as one lives life.

She was left-handed.

The thread unravels from the spool, as days spin, unused at dawn, and then, marked and used, sewn into life's pattern, life draws to its inevitable close, to its end. Life to the last drop, to the last breath…life to the spool's last yard of thread.

I have the last spool of white thread my mother gave me. I often hold it in my hand. When she gave it to me I secretly believed that as long as the spool had thread wound on it, it was tied to my mother's life. She would live. It was not so. I carried the spool of thread in my coat pocket at her funeral. There is not much left. I keep the spool in her tin box, the one with the calla lily on the lid, in my dresser, top left hand drawer.

I have many spools of thread. They form a canvas of color in that same tin box I inherited from my mother Mary. One day,

I had planned to give the tin box to my daughter and ask her to pass it on to her daughter, to tie us all together. (*Psalm 30*)

> Weeping endureth for the night
> But joy cometh in the morning

Carrie died on November 9, 2012.

When Carrie dismantled her Hawaiian home, she sent fifty cartons of "personal stuff" (her words) to a storage facility outside Los Angeles: she was certain she would live to claim her life once again. After she died, our cousin sent the boxes to my home, a few at a time, to be stored in the basement. In one of the boxes I found a dark green bound journal with two and a half pages written in her hand that stopped the unpacking for the afternoon:

ENOUGH

Be delicious

Be rare, eccentric and original

Make more mistakes

Dress to please yourself

Eat mangos naked; lick the juice off your arms

Describe yourself as marvelous

Tell the truth faster

Be inwardly outrageous

Discover your own goodness

Paint your soul

Celebrate your gorgeous friendships with women

Bathe naked by moonlight

Smile when *you* feel like it

Investigate your dark places with a flashlight

You are enough. You have enough. You do enough.

Let your creative spirit rush, flow, tumble, bubble, leak, spring, stream, dribble out of you

Weave your life into a net of love and your love and work into the net of life

ON DEATH

"My heart is sore pained within me and the terrors of death have fallen upon me. Fearfulness and trembling have come upon me. And a horror has overwhelmed me. And I said, O that I had wings like a dove, for then I would fly away and be at rest."

Carrie Hyman's journals, date unknown. Perhaps 2011.

Ruth Sidransky

Ruth Sidranksy was born in Brooklyn to two profoundly deaf parents. Her first language was Sign, and she translated the world's sounds for her parents throughout their lives.

In 1990, Sidransky wrote <u>In Silence</u>, a memoir of her life among the world of the Deaf. Nominated for a Pulitzer Prize, the *New York Times* called it "…a great act of love." Sidranksy has appeared on Good Morning, America, NPR and throughout the United States and Canada, speaking on behalf of American Sign and its legitimacy as a distinct and singular language.

Currently in her 9th decade, Ruth Sidransky published three books in 2014: ***A Woman's Primer***, a look at the qualities women need to survive and thrive; ***Bravo Carrie***, her memoir of her adult daughter's struggle with cancer, and ***Reparations***, a novel about Europe just after World War II.

Sidransky divides her time between Lenox, Massachusetts and southern Florida.

The girl on the cover is Sarah,
the author's grand daughter,
She is the daughter of Carrie,
who died of cancer,
Sadly this lovely girl is in a
psychiatric hospital now at the age
of 17. (2015).
She is supposedly very strong willed
like her grand mother and both
women did not get along.

May Sarah find the help she
needs and heal !!!

She checked herself out
of the facility and lives with
a boyfriend in Dallas, Tx.

Date ?

Made in the USA
Charleston, SC
21 January 2015